WESTMINSTER
AND PIMLICO
PAST

First published 1993
by Historical Publications Ltd
32 Ellington Street, London N7 8PL
(Tel: 071-607 1628)

ISBN 0 948667 21 4

Typeset by Historical Publications Ltd
and Fakenham Photosetting

Printed in Hong Kong by
South China Printing Company

WESTMINSTER AND PIMLICO PAST

A Visual History

by
Isobel Watson

HISTORICAL PUBLICATIONS

Acknowledgements

For their co-operation, forbearance, and many useful suggestions, I owe a great debt to Margaret Swarbrick and her staff at Westminster City Archives, especially Elizabeth Cory, Roy Harrison, Alison Kenney and John Sargent. I am also most grateful to John Phillips of the Greater London Record Office and to John Fisher and his colleagues at Guildhall Library maps and prints department, for their patient assistance and advice. A book such as this can only expose a tiny fraction of the fascinating images of Westminster in their expert care.

Along the way I have also been assisted by the Bishopsgate Institute Library, the City Corporation Record Office, Guildhall Library, the Greater London Record Office, Lambeth Archives Department, Lambeth Palace Library, the prints and drawings departments of the British Museum and the Museum of London, Glasgow University Business Records Centre and the Centre for Kentish Studies at Maidstone. I was also grateful for the kindness and assistance of Alison Barnes of the Peabody Trust and Eddie Richards of the London Gas Museum of North Thames Gas. I am pleased to acknowledge the permission of the Grosvenor estate to consult their records at Westminster City Archives; and also that I have drawn on the work of the Westminster South Local History Society, especially that of June Brown and Nicholas O'Farrell, published in that Society's newsletter; and the unpublished work of William Carey, in manuscript at Westminster City Archives, for the attribution of the design of Carlisle Place and Morpeth Terrace.

I also gratefully acknowledge assistance, ideas and support in various forms from John Greenacombe, Alison McMillan, John Richardson, Amanda Short, Aileen Stanton, David Webb, David White and Sylvia Yeldham. Last but not least, my very special thanks to Ian Day, who not only read and commented on the text in draft, but (though he little knew it) provided the original inspiration for the book.

The Illustrations

Permission to use illustrations was kindly given by the following:

The City of Westminster: 1, 6, 16, 22, 27, 31, 32, 36, 38, 40, 46, 56, 58, 59, 61, 62, 65, 67, 76, 80, 82, 84, 85, 91, 100, 101, 102, 104, 108, 116, 120, 134, 136, 137, 141, 142, 152, 155, 156, 157, 160, 161, 162, 166, 167, 170, 171, 173, 174, 175, 176, 179, 180, 181, 182, 183, 184, 186
The Greater London Record Office: 28, 41, 48, 49, 68, 106, 127, 132, 133, 144, 145, 147, 177, 186, 187
The Museum of London: 29, 98, 99
The Guildhall Library, City of London: 86, 87, 109, 143, 151, 158, 168, 172, 185
National Monuments Record: 94, 125, 189

The Grosvenor Estate Holdings: 111
The House of Fraser Collection, University of Glasgow Archives: 138, 139
The Bishopsgate Institute: 146
The British Museum: 169

Other illustrations were provided by the Author, Roger Cline and Historical Publications Ltd.

The jacket illustration, by J.P. Emslie (1898) is of 'Wharves between Lambeth Bridge and the Houses of Parliament', which were demolished for the extension of the Victoria Tower Gardens. It is reproduced with the kind permission of the City of Westminster.

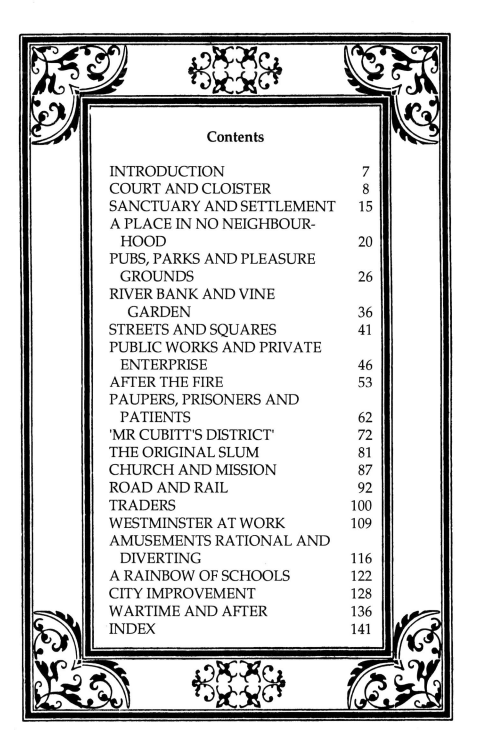

Contents

Further Reading

The best recent general account is Penelope Hunting, *Royal Westminster* (1989), prepared as an exhibition catalogue. J. E. Smith's *St John the Evangelist, Westminster: Parochial Memorials* (1892) remains useful on the subjects both of local government and topography. Gervase Rosser, *Medieval Westminster* (1989) is both scholarly and splendidly readable, and deals with St Margaret's parish between 1200 and 1540. For Pimlico, the prime text is Hermione Hobhouse's magnificent biography, *Thomas Cubitt, Master Builder* (1971).

The following is a selective list of printed material dealing with particular themes covered in the text, or which supplements them:

Barker, T. C. and Robbins, Michael, *A History of London Transport*, 2 vols. (1963)

Carleton, John D., *Westminster School: a History* (1965)

Carrington, R. *Westminster City School and its origins* (1983)

Cooke, Sir Robert, *The Palace of Westminster* (1987)

Cruickshank,Dan and Burton, Neil, *Life in the Georgian City* (1990) (Queen Anne's Gate)

Day, E. S., *An Old Westminster Foundation* (1902) (Greycoat Hospital)

Everard, Stirling, *History of the Gas Light & Coke Company* (1949)

Eyles, Allen and Skone, Keith, *London's West End Cinemas* (1991)

Griffiths, Arthur, *Memorials of Millbank* (1884) (Millbank Penitentiary)

Holland, Philip, *St Margaret's, Westminster* (1993)

Howe, Sir Ronald, *The Story of Scotland Yard* (1965)

Humble, J. G. and Peter Hansell, *Westminster Hospital* (1966)

Hyde, Ralph, *Panoramania* (1989)

Janes, Hurford, *The Red Barrel* (1963) (company history of Watney Mann)

Mander, Raymond and Mitchenson, Joe, *Theatres of London* (1975)

Mayhew, Henry, and Binney, John, *Criminal Prisons of London* (1862)

Mills, W. H. *Westminster Old and New* (1938) (real estate dealings 1898-1938)

Moss, Michael and Turton, Alison, *A Legend of Retailing* (1989) (Army and Navy Stores)

Nash, Roy, *Buckingham Palace, the Place and the People* (1980)

Port, M. H. (ed.) *The Houses of Parliament* (1976)

Percival, Alicia, *About Vincent Square* (1979)

Survey of London, volumes 10, 13 and 14: (the Parish of St. Margaret, Westminster); volume 39 (the Grosvenor estate).

Walker, R. J. B., *Old Westminster Bridge* (1979)

Whiteford-Engholm, Sylvia, *Roll-ups and Tea-cups* (1990) (life in the Old Pye Street area in the years after 1945)

Zedner, Lucia, *Women Crime and Custody in Victorian England* (1991) (Tothill Fields and Millbank prisons)

A copy of the text annotated to indicate manuscript and other sources is deposited at Westminster City Archives.

A Note about Names

Over the last century and a half many of the street names in the area have been changed, usually to prevent confusion with other streets of the same name. In some cases (such as Petty France and Broadway) the early name has been changed and later restored. Where possible, the present name is normally used in the text. In other cases, such as Duck Lane (St Matthew Street) the use of the old name recognises that the name has been changed to foster a change of character in the area.

Introduction

A single image of Westminster - the clock tower of the Palace of Westminster, always known, after the name of the bell within it, as Big Ben - is instantly recognised, all over the world, by millions who have never set foot in Europe, let alone in London. It is the pre-eminent and universal symbol of London, and indeed of the United Kingdom. The presence at Westminster, within yards of one another, of the seat of government, in London's most remarkable Victorian building; and of the Abbey, charged as it is with a thousand years of royal history, have made this one small patch of ground, a few hundred square yards, probably the most exhaustively written about of any such area of its size in the country.

When Whitehall ceased to be a royal residence, fashionable London preferred, on the whole, to relocate itself on the far side of St James's Park. As a result, though the great national institutions are themselves well-recorded, relatively little has been written about the area surrounding them. This book attempts to evoke, through pictures chosen largely from the rich collections belonging to the cities of Westminster and London, something of the flavour of the past of this neglected area. It seeks to do something towards redressing the balance, by focusing less on the Westminster known to tourists than on the Westminster known to local workers and residents, the people on whose services the running of the royal and governmental machines has always depended.

'Westminster', in different contexts, can mean areas of widely differing extent. In the middle ages, as in the borough created in 1900, it would have been understood to encompass (leaving aside a detached area in Knightsbridge) most of the land held by the medieval Abbots, stretching as far north as Oxford Street. The modern City, in 1965, even swallowed Paddington and St. Marylebone. It is however the area south of the Park, the ancient parish of St. Margaret, coextensive with the ancient village which grew up round the Abbey and the Palace, which is featured in this book. To this is added Pimlico, the triangle whose modern apex is around Victoria Station and its sides Vauxhall Bridge Road and, according to taste, either Buckingham Palace Road or Ebury Street. The tiny handful of houses and hostelries gathered round the skirts of Buckingham House, and known in the 18th century as Pimlico, grew, after Buckingham House had become Buckingham Palace and the monarch's main London residence, from a hamlet into a substantial and architecturally coherent suburb.

As with many such middle-class housing developments, of any period, early pictures of Pimlico are rare. Sensation-seeking - in the slum district closer to the Abbey which shot to notoriety in the mid-19th century - produced more visual material than quiet respectability. The respectable and the seedy; the grand and the humble, the opulent and the destitute - the overwhelming impression of the visual past of Westminster and Pimlico is one of contrasts.

Isobel Watson
July 1993

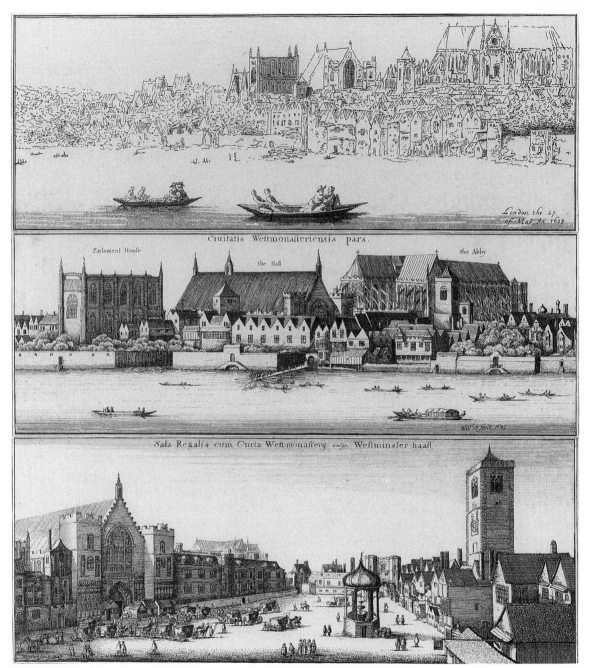

1. *17th-century views of Westminster. The uppermost, of 1625, by J.C. Keirincx, identifies the bulk of, from left to right (south to north), St Stephen's chapel of the palace of Westminster; Westminster Hall of William Rufus's New Palace of Westminster; and St Peter's Abbey. The lower images are by Wenzel (Wenceslaus) Hollar, 1647; the lowest shows New Palace Yard, its fountain and clock tower (pulled down by Wren in 1698).*

2. *The funeral of Edward the Confessor, as shown on the Bayeux Tapestry. This includes the only known depiction of the Confessor's Abbey.*

Court and Cloister

ABBEY AND PALACE

In the beginning there was an island: Thorn-ey, the island of thorns. It was marked off from the surrounding shallow marsh by subsidiary streams of the Tyburn, extending from the later site of the Abbey mill at the foot of Great College Street in the south east, directly west along that street, which marks the original line of the 'mill ditch'. In Great Smith Street the ditch divided around an island, still marked by a curve in the road. North west of Dean's Yard it continued along the medieval 'Long Ditch' (Storey's Gate), returning east somewhere north of New Palace Yard. In the tenth century Thorney is described as an awesome place, although probably less on account of its appearance than of the story (devised perhaps out of rivalry with St Paul's in the City of London) that the consecration of the Abbey, established more than two centuries earlier, was attended by none other than a ghostly St Peter.

The importance of Westminster, the westerly and later rival of St Paul's, as a royal and hence a national site and symbol, is owed not to propaganda or the promotion of superstition, but to the piety of Edward the Confessor. St Peter's Abbey had become a Benedictine foundation in the tenth century, while Dunstan was Bishop of London, and was rebuilt and enlarged by Edward in the eleventh, to represent the

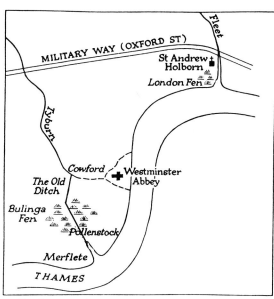

3. *Sketch map to show the probable course of two arms of the river Tyburn as they formed Thorney Island by the Thames. The enclosed area is now roughly that of Parliament Square and the Abbey and Palace of Westminster.*

height of Norman artistry and technology. At his death the Abbey was all but complete. The Norman kings who followed were to consolidate its importance, and by further rebuilding endeavoured to establish a firm link between an Abbey coronation

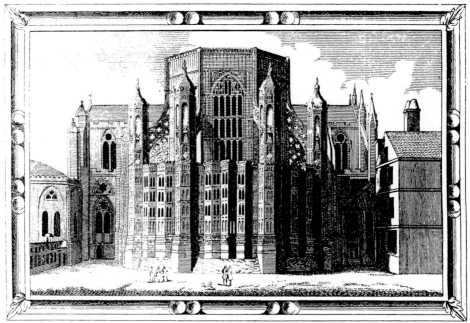

4. *The Henry VII Chapel of Westminster Abbey. From Chamberlain's* New and Compleat History and Survey of the Cities of London and Westminster...*(1770).*

5. *The north front of Westminster Hall, by Michael Rooker (1770s). This view illustrates well the cluster of taverns and coffee-houses around the Hall. The western towers of the Abbey, visible in the background, were added by Hawksmoor between 1732 and 1745.*

6. *New Palace Yard, c1832. This watercolour by Anne Rickman (the daughter of John Rickman, a Parliamentary clerk), shows the old Exchequer Buildings, her own house (formerly Horace Walpole's residence) at the north-east corner, and, next to it, the Star Chamber.*

and the legitimacy of the succession. The nave and chapter-house represent the work of the reign of Henry III, who fostered the cult of the Confessor as a place of national pilgrimage just as he obliterated much of the Confessor's church. The Tudors affirmed the royal connection, as Henry's own Lady chapel gave way to Henry VII's magnificent replacement, intended as Henry VI's monument, a royal burial-place, and once again a link between a disputed succession and a hallowed past.

The neighbouring palace, closer to the river east of Old Palace Yard, had become the principal seat of the court, and thus of government, by the reign of Canute. William Rufus began a new palace, of which only Westminster Hall (opening on to New Palace Yard) survives, re-roofed by Richard II. Out of the royal councils grew the modern parliaments. The 'model' Parliament of Edward I was held in Westminster Hall, but thereafter the Lords and Commons met separately, the Lords in the palace itself but the Commons for three centuries finding their home in the Abbey chapter-house. It was only in 1540, after Henry VIII had finally abandoned the palace of Westminster as a royal seat, that they were enabled to return, establishing a permanent home in St Stephen's chapel. By the time of its virtual destruction by fire in October 1834 the medieval palace of Westminster

7. *The Coronation Banquet of James II, 1685, in Westminster Hall. It is set beneath Hugh Herland's glorious roof and against Henry Yevele's south window, constructed during the remodelling of the Hall in the 1390s under Richard II.*

had become a miscellaneous jumble of Parliamentary and government offices, adapted and rebuilt over the centuries.

THE PALACE OF WHITEHALL

Along the riverside between Westminster and the village of Charing stood residences built by powerful interests seeking to be close to the Tudor court. To the north was the London residence of the kings of Scotland or their ambassadors, later known as Scotland Yard. It was eventually absorbed into its southerly neighbour, York Place, residence of the Archbishops of York.

The Palace of Westminster, already a ramshackle ruin, was badly damaged by fire in 1512. Henry VIII, a frequent visitor at York Place, saw his Cardinal Archbishop rebuilding his mansion in magnificent style and taste. Henry's expropriation in 1529 of Wolsey's lands signalled the removal of the court to York Place, renamed Whitehall. During the next century and a half building, rebuilding and enlargement of the new palace proceeded on a piecemeal basis, producing a vast and rambling complex spanning both sides of the rutted and ruinous road. Latterly called King Street, the road linked the pal-

aces of Whitehall and Westminster. On the east side of the street were the royal apartments, ranged round an old orchard redeveloped as a formal courtyard called the Privy Garden. On the west Henry acquired the lands formerly belonging to the leper hospital of St James, and laid out a tilt-yard for bear-baiting and tournaments, a cockpit and more than one tennis court. The two sides of the palace grounds were linked, from 1530, by gatehouses at each end of the street, separating Westminster's King Street from the broader expanse of Whitehall to the north. Through the northern gatehouse, called by tradition the Holbein Gate, it was possible to pass from one side of the palace to the other, above ground level.

By the time of the Commonwealth the palace was a virtual warren, containing some two thousand rooms, many of them let as lodgings to individual courtiers and officials, a practice which continued after the restoration of Charles II. As at Westminster, fire was a regular foe, all the more intractable for the diversity of the occupants. A fire in 1618 generated plans for comprehensive rebuilding, resulting principally in Inigo Jones's new banqueting house, which was in use by 1623. Although the palace rules required a bucket by every chimney, nothing was

8. Old Palace Yard, looking north, etched by J.T. Smith and based on a painting by Canaletto.

proof against the final conflagration of 1698, said to have been started when a Dutch lodger left her washing carelessly close to the coals. The devastation was such that little, apart from the Banqueting House and some buildings round the Privy Garden, survived. The Dutch King and his Queen, disliking Whitehall's riverside climate, had departed for Kensington and Hampton Court. There was, therefore, little incentive to rebuild, and today small portions of reconstructed wall, and Tudor wine vaults below the Ministry of Defence buildings, are all that remain of the fabric of Whitehall before the days of the Stuarts.

9. *Whitehall Yard, leading (on the right), to Scotland Yard, with part of the Banqueting House, 1766; drawn by Paul Sandby.*

10. *Westminster 1658, from the map by William Faithorne.*

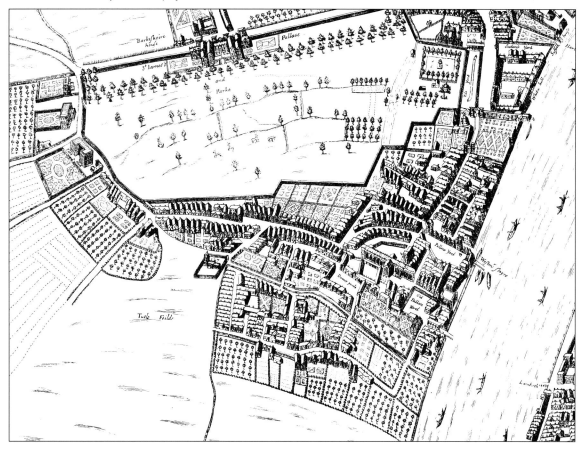

11. *The so-called Holbein Gate, at the northern entrance to Whitehall Palace. Built in 1530, it stood just south of the Banqueting House. Regarded in the 18th century as one of the 'greatest curiosities in London', it survived until 1759.*

12. *The King Street Gate, at the south end of Whitehall Palace, level with Downing Street. Built at the same time as the northern gate, it was demolished in 1723.*

13. *A Perspective View of the Privy Garden, Whitehall, 1741, looking south towards the House. Drawn by J. Maurer.*

Sanctuary and Settlement

THE TOWN OF WESTMINSTER

The medieval Abbey claimed a royal grant of land extending east from its walls almost to the city walls of London, north to what is now Oxford Street and west to Knightsbridge. The southern part of this area, below Charing Cross, became (together with a detached area around Knightsbridge) the medieval parish of St Margaret's. But the settlement generated by monastery and monarchs was relatively small. By the time of Henry VIII's seizure of the Abbey lands in 1540 it extended little further west than Petty France, and to the north was blocked by the sprawl of the palace of Whitehall just beyond Channel Row, now Cannon Row. To the south of the Abbey gardens and a handful of houses off Tothill Street lay the boggy waste of Tothill Fields, to the north west Henry VIII's deer park of St James.

The entrance to the Fields lay from the broad way at the west end of Tothill Street. Much effort has gone into debating the site of the original Tot- or lookout hill. The name Tothill dates from no later than the 12th century, not from 17th century fortifications in the Fields, and the hill was probably to be found in the village itself, most likely at a slight rise in the ground at the west end of 'the great way of Tothill', near what is now called St Ermin's Hill. Though no hill, not even a bump, has survived the building of the District Railway and massive mansion blocks, this site was sufficiently eminent to be chosen at some unidentified medieval date for a chapel to St Armel, a dragon-slaying Welsh saint esteemed during the 15th century. The saint's name was much mangled (St Hermit, St Dormer and St Torment, for example) in later times.

The Abbey had a substantial number of lay servants, and the shrine of St Edward attracted pilgrims. The palace, as well as its permanent establishment of royal retainers, drew a transient population of litigants, lawgivers and those who would now be called lobbyists. Wool merchants dealt at the Woolstaple (on the present site of Bridge Street) and purveyors of furs and cloth at the fair of St Edward, established by Henry III and originally held in the churchyard of St Margaret's. These must have included a substantial number of foreigners, as the name of Petty France,

14. The corner of Tothill Street and Broadway, c1850. The medieval house is typical of the streetscape of Tothill Street until the later 19th century.

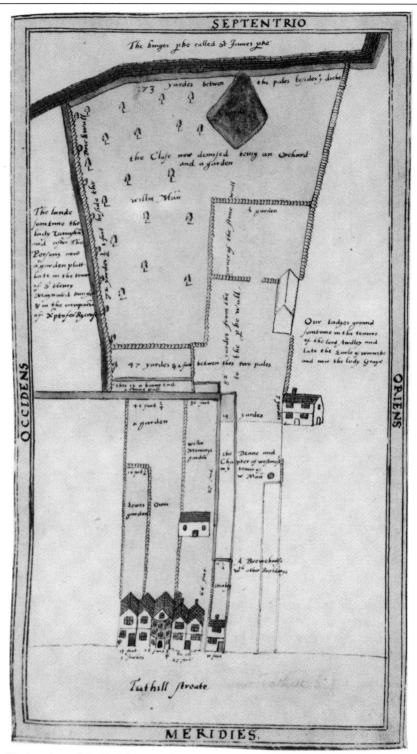

15. *Ralph Treswell's plan of part of the Christ's Hospital estate, given to the Hospital by Richard Castell in 1556. To the north is St James's Park (the large pond approximates to the site of the later cockpit). To the south, Tothill Street.*

16. *Medieval houses in King Street between Little Sanctuary and Bow Street ('Thieving Lane'). Pen and wash drawing 1798, possibly by J.T. Smith.*

17. *Caxton's house in Westminster, from an 1827 engraving. A house traditionally associated with Caxton was demolished in the 1820s; the remains of the Almonry gave way to Victoria Street c1850.*

18. *Caxton's printer's mark, late 15th century.*

19. *South east view of the entrances to Little Sanctuary and Thieving Lane, from King Street. Drawn by J.T. Smith 1807. Grindstones are at the corner of the central building, which was an ironmonger's shop.*

20. *Little Sanctuary from the west. 'This place which was once an asylum for fugitive offenders is at this time a harbour for wretchedness, filth and contagion.' Drawing by J.T. Smith, early 19th century.*

first recorded in 1494, suggests. To all of these the medieval village provided a service economy. Trades, victualling and the provision of fruit and nursery plants were to be found in premises developed by those granted leases of land by the different administrative departments of the Abbey, which was by far the largest landlord. Thus an area south of Tothill Street, which was the province of the almoner or alms-giver, came to be known as the Almonry. Here William Caxton's printing business, and that of his successor Wynkyn de Worde, flourished at the 'sign of the red pale' in the last quarter of the 15th century.

At the western gate of the Abbey was the sanctuary. From the early middle ages the monks asserted a right to give safe harbour to alleged criminals, beyond the jurisdiction of the civil courts, a right which was later extended to debtors, but exercised beyond the inner precinct of the Abbey itself. The concept of sanctuary survived the dissolution of the religious houses but was not completely done away with until the reign of James I. By this time the presence of a community of lawbreakers, actual and presumed, had done nothing for the reputation of the area close to the Abbey.

Westminster had become a large village, or small town, home to the entire spectrum of society from the king to the common criminal. Tothill Street and Petty France had comfortable houses for the comfortably off. To the north of the Sanctuary lay a bow-shaped lane called Bow Street, or Thieving Lane, which tells its own story. To the west of King Street lay a dense network of courts and alleys.

21. *Eastern entrance to Thieving Lane, drawn by J.T. Smith in 1808 during redevelopment of the Middlesex Guildhall area.*

22. *The Gatehouse prison, originally a 14th-century project by the Abbey cellarer. This stood until 1776 at the top of Tothill Street, where now a granite column of 1861 commemorates the former Westminster scholars who died in the Crimean wars.*

23. *St Margaret's church, 1750.*

CHURCH AND PARISH

St Margaret's Westminster was a large parish, co-extensive with the 13th century Abbey estate, extending eastward to its boundary with St Clement Danes, and westward to include the manor of Knightsbridge. The parish of St Martin in the Fields was carved out in the 14th century. In 1548 Henry VIII added to St Martin's the part of St Margaret's which lay north of his new palace of Whitehall, to avoid the inconvenience and hazard of plague-struck parishioners' corpses being brought through the palace by road for burial. The parishes of St Paul Covent Garden, St James Piccadilly and St Anne Soho were separately constituted in the 17th century, and St George Hanover Square (comprising Mayfair and what became Pimlico) in 1725, followed closely by St John the Evangelist.

The present church of St Margaret's, built over some forty years from about 1487 by prosperous parishioners with support from the Abbey, is the third on the site. To this period dates the famous east window, which is believed to have been made for Henry VIII, and which reached Westminster only in the mid-18th century, a period when substantial building works to the exterior, especially the tower, were taking place. Until the early 19th century the eastern part of the churchyard was cluttered with small tenements. The churchyard was the original site for the medieval fair of St Edward established by Henry III; later churchwardens raised income by letting space for the building of raised seating for spectators at great ceremonial occasions such as coronations and royal funerals. One of the earliest burials in the present church, in 1491, was that of William Caxton. The 17th century brought the interments of Sir Walter Raleigh; of Wenzel (Wenceslaus) Hollar, the engraver to whom we owe so much of what we know of the London of his time; and of Alexander Davies, ancestor of the Grosvenor fortune, whose restored tomb is the only one remaining in the churchyard, out of over a thousand counted in the mid-19th century. Also from the 17th century, monuments commemorate the local benefactors Cornelius van Dun, Emery Hill and James Palmer. Milton and his first wife were married here, as were Samuel and Elizabeth Pepys.

In 1605, the parish made a special payment to its bellringers for their efforts in 'ringing at the tyme when the Parlement howse should have been blown upp'. This prefigures the later distinction of the church as the 'national church of the House of Commons'. This link is usually traced to the communion held here, on the opening of a new Parliament in 1614. For the first time, in that year, St Margaret's was chosen for this purpose instead of the Abbey, out of Puritan distaste for High Church practice; thus a new tradition was born. Though the nature of the link (like that of St Margaret's with the Abbey itself) has altered over the centuries - the House ceased in the mid-19th century to appoint preachers, and to hold regular 'state services' - its special relationship with the House has enabled the parish to call from time to time on Exchequer funds for repair, restoration and improvement.

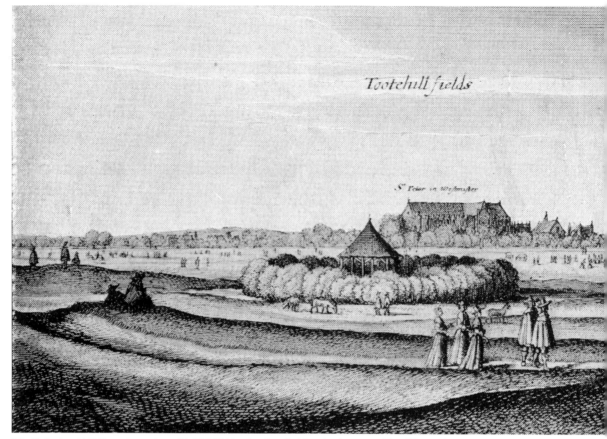

Tootehill fields

S.t Peter in Westminster

24. *Hollar's mid-17th century view of Tothill Fields, showing the Maze in the centre. The Abbey and Westminster Hall are seen in the middle distance.*

A Place in No Neighbourhood

THE SOUTHERN FIELDS

The fields lying south and west of Westminster seem to have acquired the name Tothill, by association with Tothill Street, by the mid-16th century. Along the river bank and around the Neat Houses lay market gardens, described at the beginning of the 18th century as supplying London with asparagus, artichokes, cauliflowers, musk melons and other exotic vegetables. Otherwise the southern fields seem to have been waste ground, and so marshy that as late as the 1820s it was possible, according to some accounts, to go duck-shooting here.

A curious early pleasure resort was a maze, renovated at parish expense in 1672. This is probably the subject of Hollar's drawing at illustration 24. Until the early 19th century accounts of the fields are almost unreservedly bleak. Jeremy Bentham is reported as saying, as late as 1798, "if a place could exist in no neighbourhood, that place would be Tothill Fields". The characterisation almost became true. After the establishment of the parish of St John the Evangelist in the 18th century, Tothill Fields was left a place apart, beyond the clear responsibility of either St Margaret's or St John's vestry.

It was a natural enough spot to choose for a ground to set up butts for shooting practice, now commemorated merely in the name of Artillery Row. A 'shooting-house' here, near what was then the built-up limit of urban Westminster, was provided at the south-western end of Tothill Street in 1661, out of a legacy from one John Allen. In later times, when the memory of civil war had faded, it became a bowling-green.

Before 1612 St Margaret's parish established, at a spot close to where today Douglas Place joins Vauxhall Bridge Road, a group of dwellings known as the pest houses, later as the Five Chimneys. These af-

bear-baiting, or any excuse for betting, when tempers tended to rise and violence follow. Fairs offering this kind of diversion lost popularity in the early 19th century, and were suppressed altogether about 1840. At the best of times the fields were associated with robbers and footpads.

Marking the southern boundary of Tothill Fields was one branch of the Tyburn, on its route from Hampstead via Marylebone to the river. Later this became known as the King's Scholars' pond sewer, from a long-disappeared 'shaggy pool, deep enough to drown a horse', a favoured haunt of the anglers among the Westminster schoolboys. In the early 19th century there was, on the site of Lillington Gardens, a slaughteryard for horses. The burn, or sewer, is today traced above ground by the line of Tachbrook Street. (There was, however, never a Tach brook. Mid-19th century street names in this locality refer to parts of Warwickshire associated with the landowner, Henry Wise, a royal gardener who acquired property here in the late 17th century.)

The Willow Walk (now Warwick Way) divided extensive reed beds to the north from the market gardens which extended all the way to the river. This footway to Chelsea was joined more effectively to Westminster after 1677, when Rochester Row was formed, the linked thoroughfares being blocked to wheeled traffic by felled tree-trunks used as stiles. Financed by a bequest from Emery Hill, the causeway of Rochester Row (so named from the traditional association of the Deanery of Westminster with the bishopric of Rochester) was lined with ninety elm trees, and Emery Hill's almshouses (illustration 84) were the first buildings to front the new way, on its northern side.

Beyond Rochester Row, around and beyond the Willow Walk, lay the fields of the ancient manor of

forded a kind of quarantine for plague victims. This provision was quite inadequate, of course, in the plague year of 1665, when it was augmented by wooden sheds. No parish charity could have coped with disaster of such a scale, nor could any parish churchyard. Some 3,000 plague victims were buried in that year by St Margaret's, many of them, according to tradition, in the Fields.

The Fields are said also to have served as a burial ground when Cromwell's wretched army of Scots prisoners were quartered here after the battle of Worcester. Tradition also has it that those that were not sold into slavery in the West Indies - some 1,200 - died and were buried here. The sheer number of alleged burials make it surprising that there are not more accounts such as that of the discovery of ten skeletons in the grounds of the Greycoat Hospital in 1886.

In the 18th century, duellists chose Tothill Fields as a remote spot where they were unlikely to be troubled by the law. At other times, especially holidays, crowds would assemble for horse-racing, bull- and

25. Duelling with pistols in Tothill Fields, 1711. Sir Cholmondely Dearing's death from close-range fire from Sir Richard Thornhill.

26. *Tothill Fields in 1807. There is a drainage ditch in the marshy ground here in the foreground of the picture. The horse and cart are proceeding along Horseferry Road to the Thames. The viewpoint is approximately from the centre of modern Rochester Row looking towards the Greycoat School and the backs of the houses in Great Peter Street. Aquatint by Arnald and Fellows.*

27. *Scholars skating on the ice near the pest houses on Tothill Fields.*

28. *A 19th-century watercolour of the pest houses in Tothill Fields.*

29. *Boys fishing in a pond at Tothill Fields, c1840, by J.H. Mole.*

30. *The ferry house at the horse ferry. The ferry service fell into decline during the building of Westminster Bridge (opened in 1750), but until Lambeth Bridge was built this remained a natural place to take a hired boat.*

Eia, extending to the boundary of Chelsea parish formed by the Westbourne. In the midst of these fields lay the farm of Ey-bury, at the very south-west end of what is now the Buckingham Palace Road. A nearby farm was Neate, the area of the modern Sutherland Row becoming known as the Neat Houses. The extensive and productive market gardens, which stretched all the way to the river, acquired the name of Neat House gardens by association. Beyond the Neat Houses, a natural inlet of the Thames was developed after 1722 as a reservoir by the Chelsea Water Works Company, which ultimately supplied most of Westminster with water piped through hollowed elm logs.

MILLBANK

Millbank takes its name from the Abbey mill, which stood as late as 1650 at the foot of Great College Street. The mill ditch ran west along Great College Street, divided around a small island now traced by the curve in Great Smith Street, and ran along the line of Orchard Street before turning at a right angle down Strutton Ground towards the horse ferry. The river bank was probably raised as a flood prevention measure, floods being no small risk. Until 1656, when the parish accepted responsibility for its maintenance, the bank was in poor repair, as a result of a

dispute with the Archbishop of Canterbury, the owner of the rights to the ferry.

The ferry was operated on what would now be called a franchise basis. In the 16th century the Archbishop granted the lucrative rights to yeomen of Lambeth, usually for the duration of two named lives. Later grantees, described as gentlemen, either underleased their rights to the ferry, or employed others to man the flat-bottomed punts, which were large enough to carry a coach and six. The economic importance of the ferry was such that in the years round 1700 five young ferrymen were given special exemption from being pressed into the navy. The ferrymen were, like coach drivers, known for their rude manners and foul language. The service deteriorated once Westminster Bridge neared completion, and the boats were allowed to fall into disrepair.

South of the horse ferry lay the 'market meadows' where the medieval Monday market of Westminster is said to have been held, although if this is so the waterlogged nature of the ground must have made it a damp and unpleasant affair.

As with the Fields, so with Millbank. Even in broad daylight the pedestrian along Millbank was at risk from attack, such that in the 18th century St John's vestry employed a Sunday watchman as an escort for churchgoers walking from the riverside.

31. *A cottage on Millbank, drawn by J.T. Smith and published in 1797.*

32. *Still rural Westminster. A cow which had escaped from 'the neighbourhood of Horseferry Road', leaping the gates of Sir Robert Peel's residence in Whitehall Gardens, c1848.*

Pubs, Parks and Pleasure Grounds

TAVERNS OF THE TOWN

Westminster was famous for its taverns. King Street was notorious: in the mid-16th century 58 are recorded between Tothill Street and Charing Cross and in 1585 the local burgesses attempted to restrict the number in St Margaret's to 60. By the mid-18th century, around two hundred publicans' licences would be renewed in an average year for the area between Rochester Row, the horse ferry and Scotland Yard.

By this time there were some thirty taverns in King Street alone. In Tothill Street and Petty France, which offered better access for coach traffic from the west, were several inns with coaching yards. Tradition attributes to the Cock (illustration 34), in a large yard on the north side of Tothill Street, the function of being the counting house for the wages of the 13th century workmen rebuilding the Abbey. Whatever the truth of that, certainly an inn called the Cock and Tabard existed in Tothill Street in the time of Henry VII.

Other drinking places abounded. Pepys we know to have frequented at least twelve identified taverns in King Street alone, and several curiously-named dives near the Palace of Westminster - Heaven, outside Westminster Hall; Hell facing New Palace Yard, and Purgatory.

Duplication of some of their names has led to a degree of confusion about the ancient taverns. The Black Horse, notably, was a meeting place for the brutish gang of horse- and deer-thieves with whom the equally unpleasant Dick Turpin consorted, and the scene where they met in 1735 to plan a burglary at Edgware - the incident which led to the breaking of the gang, and sent Turpin into hiding. This Black Horse tavern stood in Broadway, and disappeared earlier than the public house of the same name which stood (until replaced about 1902 by the Buckingham Arms) in Petty France.

It is usually difficult to be certain that there is identity, over the years, between a name and a place, and practically all the old pubs whose signs survive have been rebuilt. Nevertheless, there has been a Star (later the Star and Crown) in Broadway since the 1730s, and a Red Lion in Parliament Street since the street was created in the 1750s. The Two Chairmen in Dartmouth Street is often identified as the oldest Westminster pub business; the sign can be traced to 1729, and its then licensee, William Swain, for some

33. The Blue Boar's Head, King Street,1858, by T.H. Shepherd .

ten years before that. The Adam and Eve in Petty France can also be traced to 1729. No business of this age, however, retains its original premises. The oldest surviving pub structure is now a private house: no. 6 Barton Street was the Salutation Inn (the sign representing the appearance of the angel to Mary) virtually from its construction in the 1720s until it became a lodging house about 1890. Still in the licensed business however is the early Victorian building of the Elephant and Castle in Great Peter Street, which replaces a Castle pub in existence in 1729.

SPORTS

Cock-fighting had the dignity, in the eighteenth century, of the so-called 'royal' cockpit, which was depicted by Hogarth in the 1750s and Rowlandson some fifty years later. It stood until 1815 on the fringe of the Park - having moved there from the precinct of Whitehall Palace to the foot of the Cockpit steps from Dartmouth Street. Though it is said by that time to have been long disused, tradition also has it that the 'sport' became re-established about 1821 in Tufton Street, no doubt contributing to the street's unsalubrious character. There were also dog-fighting establishments. In 1792 one William Ebberfield (probably the same individual as a well-known local criminal called Slender Billy, later hanged for forgery) was prosecuted by his neighbours for the nui-

34. *The Cock Tavern, Tothill Street, in 1807. Pen and wash drawing by C.W. Dempsey.*

35. *The Royal Cockpit, Birdcage Walk, by Rowlandson and Pugin, 1808.*

36. *A dog-fight in the Westminster Pit, 1821. An etching by 'an amateur'.*

sance caused by dog- and badger-baiting in a house in Great Peter Street. In another (or perhaps the same) 'pit', said to be in Duck Lane, then the heart of the Westminster slums, a dog-fighting African monkey attracted the fashionable West End, to rub shoulders with more local low life.

THEATRES AND TEA GARDENS

There were places of resort of a gentler, more rural character. Pepys occasionally visited gardens at the Neat Houses, although complaining of the rough, ready and limited nature of the available refreshment ("nothing but a bottle of wine to be had"). Some horticultural establishments provided refreshments as a sideline. Among several pubs which surrounded the horse ferry, the present White Horse and Bower in Horseferry Road replaces an earlier White Horse, set back further from the road and run from about 1742 by a publican turned market gardener called Francis Fleet, on what he called 'the Mulberry Garden'. The 'Bower' represents a garden arbour constructed behind the pub by a later proprietor, about 1800.

The easiest way to the Neat Houses was by water, but from 1677 walking became easier with the addition of Rochester Row to the causeway along Warwick Way. Before reaching the wooden Ebury Bridge over the northern end of the Chelsea reservoir, the mid-18th century traveller to Chelsea would have encountered at least four pubs, the best-remembered a garden and drinking-house by the eccentric name of the Whim, or Jenny's Whim. Its speciality consisted in the theatrical effects achieved when a visitor, strolling amongst the ponds and flower-beds, happened by the unwitting pressure of his or her foot - to release a hidden spring. Out from the bushes would burst a painted effigy, representing some grotesque animal, or theatrical character. Before long this novelty faded, though a rival establishment close by, the so-called Monster tavern, originally set apart at the north-east end of what became Sutherland Row, continued as a tea garden into the 19th century (illustration 38). Although there have been attempts to attribute this almost equally curious name to the ancient presence of 'monastery' farms in the area, it is much more likely that it reflected the presence of weird contraptions similar to those at the Whim. The Gun tavern, in Buckingham Gate, is said (until its removal in 1857 for the redevelopment of the area) to have had similar curiosities in its grounds.

37. The wooden bridge (known originally as Chelsea Bridge, on the site of the modern Ebury Bridge) leads towards Jenny's Whim and the Neat Houses.

38. The Monster Tavern, north-east of the present Sutherland Row, by T.H. Shepherd, 1857.

39. The rear garden of the Gun Tavern, Buckingham Gate, by T.H. Shepherd, 1857.

PIMLICO AND RUMBILLO

The area immediately south west of Buckingham Gate (then St James's Street) was known for two hundred years, from the 1620s, as Pimlico. (The name seems to have been borrowed from a well-known public house, on the City fringe in Hoxton, purveying 'ale and cakes' and established around the end of the previous century.) The mid-18th century neighbourhood called Pimlico contained more than a dozen taverns and several coffee houses. These were clustered round Buckingham House, as it was then, and a nearby mansion, belonging to the Earls of Stafford and curiously known as Tart Hall, which was demolished in the 1720s. The Stag brewery, established by the 1640s where Stag Place now stands, was in the early 19th century still described as situated in Pimlico. The name may simply owe its origin to the area's character as a resort, or associations with a special type of brew. The earliest pub still in this quarter, the name though not the building traceable to the 1790s, is the curiously named Bag o' Nails. Classicists used to like to think this was a corruption of 'Bacchanals' - but pubs were not, generally speaking, named from the classics. The name Pimlico, of course, has been completely displaced, appropriated by the early Victorian suburb to the south west of the original area.

A name also associated with a cluster of pubs, but which has completely disappeared, is the even more curious Rumbillo. This denoted the district from the foot of Ebury Street (also known as Ebury or Avery farm), extending a short way along what is now Pimlico Road and was then the road to the Ranelagh pleasure grounds in Chelsea. The direct route to the pleasure gardens would be a natural enough place to attract publicans. (The name itself seems to derive from a local field name, Rumbelowes, but to have been popularised through association with Strombolo House which stood on the present site of 77-79 Pimlico Road, opposite another famous Chelsea resort, the Bun House.) This group of pubs numbered around ten in the 1750s. The Flask, with its skittle alley, stood in Ebury Square till about 1868. The Orange, or Royal Orange, coffee house, tea garden and latterly private theatre, was displaced by St Barnabas church. The name survives in the pub opposite. (Another private theatre, the Westminster, stood near the Park at the entrance to Queen Anne's Gate: illustration 41.)

The Ranelagh gardens closed in 1803, but their name was taken over, from about 1809 onwards, by New Ranelagh, an imitator on a smaller scale, sited near the river between the present lines of Ranelagh Road and Claverton Street. Here, in the twenty remaining years before industrial production engulfed this area, were held balls, concerts, firework displays and sailing contests. During this period the existing riverside pub called the William IV had a predecessor, somewhat to the north.

40. Interior of the Royal Orange Theatre, south of the present Pimlico Road, 1832.

41. *The interior of the original Westminster Theatre, near Queen Anne's Gate, in June 1832. The modern Westminster Theatre inhabits a converted chapel in Palace Street.*

ST JAMES'S PARK

Henry VIII drained and enclosed St James's Park and added it to the royal demesne to enhance his palace of Whitehall. The 12th-century charitable foundation of St James originally housed, on the northern side of this extensive meadowland, a retreat for female lepers. By the early 16th century, with an establishment limited to four almswomen, none apparently diseased, it had, through scandalous mismanagement and neglect, become what has been described as 'a retirement home for the relatively well to do'. Other than introducing game and rebuilding St James's Palace, Henry VIII seems to have done little more with the land than establish his sports complex on the west of Whitehall. James I took a greater interest in a four-acre field west of the Park, where he fostered an abortive experiment in planting mulberry trees to feed silk worms. It was not until the restoration of the Stuarts that anything like the modern Park emerged. The rough pasture was swiftly transformed into a formal landscape in the height of French fashion. The layout of the canal (for which the Doge and Senate of Venice presented gondolas and the tree-lined avenue

of the Mall, which now forms the northern boundary, are, somewhat uncertainly, attributed to the French designer Le Notre. Little is established about the history of the Park between this time and the early 19th century. Even the water at the western end, long called Rosamond's Pond until filled in about 1771, cannot be associated with any identifiable Rosamond. But the Park's early years under the restored monarchy are well documented by its users. For example, both Pepys and Evelyn were fascinated by virtuoso skating, in the icy December of 1662, on remarkable iron and steel contraptions newly imported from the Netherlands.

Another source of fascination were the exotic birds, to which the inhabitants of the Whitehall Palace 'volary' were added. Evelyn noted a pelican, "a fowl between a stork and a swan; a melancoly waterfowl, brought from Astracan by the Russian Ambassador; a milk-white raven; two Balearian cranes - one of which, having had his legs broken, and cut off above the knee, had a wooden or boxen leg and thigh, with a joint so accurately made that the creature could walk and use it as well as if it had been natural..."'There were also parrots, cassowaries, several kinds of deer, elk, and 'Arabian sheep'. William III was an admirer

42. A plan of St James's Park, by Knyff, c1662. Le Notre's canal took advantage of a naturally waterlogged area. To the east can be seen the locations of the Tudor cockpit and tilt-yard.

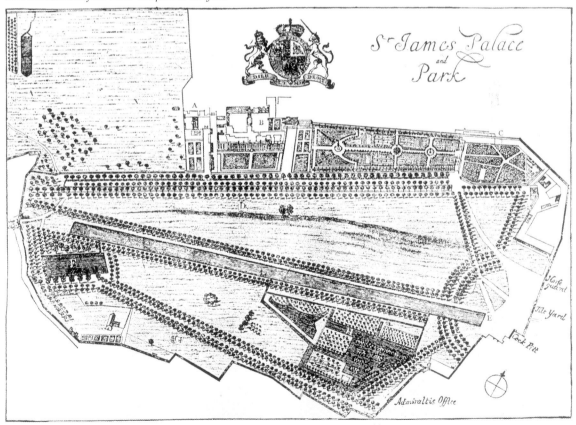

43. *The Mall, c1745. Looking west towards Buckingham House; in the foreground a soldier is on guard duty. Drawn by Chatelain.*

44. *Skating on the canal near Buckingham House, 1817.*

of the indigenous bird-life, and had a special hut constructed on what was called 'Duck Island'. Charles II is said to have jocularly conferred the title of Governor of this part of the royal territories on more than one of his associates.

It was usually open to the public to walk in the Park, though to the irritation of the 17th-century diarists the King would close it, unannounced, often for reasons of his own security. A century later, though nominally access was by means of a key, there were thousands of keys in circulation, and low life abounded. Boswell, living in Downing Street, regarded the Park as the obvious place for picking up young women, and his contemporaries with different tastes found Birdcage Walk equally fruitful for meeting young men. In August 1814 revels in the park were held, prematurely as it turned out, to celebrate the defeat of Napoleon.

Just as Henry VIII had recognised the value of the Park to enjoyment of his palace, the newly crowned George IV wished to see the formal French landscape, neglected and degraded, remodelled in the style of his own inimitable John Nash, who was rebuilding his palace at the western end. On this spot James I's mulberry garden (itself a resort of no good repute in the 17th century) had accommodated the building of first, Goring House (for the Earl of Norwich), replaced after a fire by an extravagant pile built by the Earl of Arlington. This in its turn was replaced by the Duke of Buckingham, and it was his house, the third on the site, which became in 1763 the family home of George III and Queen Charlotte. As Prince Regent, their son had hated it, but having concluding it was more regal than his own Carlton House, in the 1820s he had it virtually rebuilt at public expense, and the Park redesigned to complement it. Nash retained the central canal, but reshaped it and landscaped its banks, so that it is his semi-formal park, pelicans included, that remains one of London's best loved public parks today.

46. 'M. Chevalier de Moret's aerostatic machine', or 'the Pimlico balloon', advertised to take off from the area south west of Buckingham Palace in August 1784. The crowd were disappointed, and a riot ensued, leading to difficulties for Vincent Lunardi and his more scientific apparatus, the first to become successfully airborne in England (at the Royal Artillery Ground in Finsbury) the following month.

47. James Boswell, published by William Daniell, 1808.

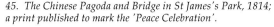

45. The Chinese Pagoda and Bridge in St James's Park, 1814; a print published to mark the 'Peace Celebration'.

Petterborough house

48. *Millbank in the 1670s, from an engraving by Hollar. On the extreme left, Peterborough House; in the middle distance Tart Hall and Goring House (destroyed by fire in 1674), on the site of Buckingham Palace. To the right, the development of the Millbank wharves and the Abbey Vine Garden.*

River Bank and Vine Garden

THE VINE GARDEN

By the second decade of the 17th century the urban population was expanding southwards from Tothill Street and the Almonry. Thus Great Peter Street, originally no more than a footway from St Peter's Abbey along Millbank and westward to the Fields, began at this time to be bordered by houses and gardens.

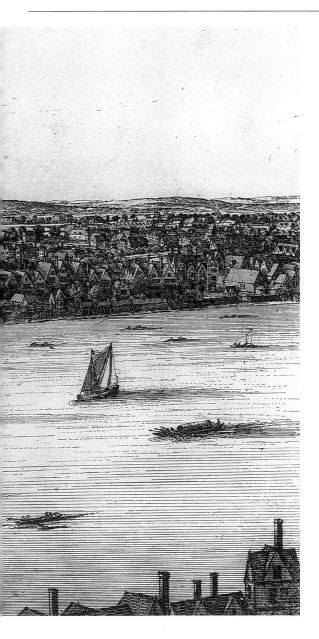

House', as Dacre House became, came to be known as Sturton Meadow, or Strutton Ground. Its land seems to have lain on either side of Abbey Orchard Street, and may have comprised the site of Old Pye Street, built on property which by the mid-17th century belonged to the Parliamentarian, Sir Robert Pye. The east side of Strutton Ground began to be developed about 1616, and was a line of small houses by 1620. Until the end of the century they had a clear view across the mill ditch. After 1661 the foreground was occupied by the Artillery Ground.

South of Great Peter Street, between Horseferry Road and the river, lay the eight acres of the Abbey vine garden. This land, a perquisite of the royal laundresses during the Tudor period, also descended from the Dacres to the Sackvilles. The only part not planted with trees in the mid-17th century, apart from reed-beds on Millbank, was around the alley called Laundry Yard (now obliterated by the mass of No. 2 Marsham Street). Another early street, called the Bowling Alley, built on what had been the abbey 'Ostrey' (hostelry) garden, is now the northern limb of Tufton Street. Development of Great Peter Street (its eastern limb called Wood Street after the two brothers who first built there) began about 1621. Gradually the neighbourhood of the horse ferry was also built over. A substantial area, now stretching from Medway Street to Tufton Street, remained to descend through a Sackville marriage to a Tufton. Land between Millbank and Tufton Street was acquired by Simon Smith and his son Henry, and the remainder passed to the Marsham family of the Mote, Maidstone. Hollar's engraving of about 1674 (illustration 48) shows the riverside heavily developed with barge-boarded buildings, and the backs of wharf property, all of it constructed in the previous twenty years.

The one-time Vine Garden became market garden, mostly remaining as such until the early 19th century. A property leased as a hop yard in 1620 is still commemorated by the name of Bennet's Yard, the passage between Marsham and Tufton Streets. By the beginning of the 18th century the acres of the Vine Garden boasted only a handful of buildings, those in Wood Street barge-boarded and "ready to fall".

Vine Street (now part of Romney Street) was described as "a pretty handsome open place"; facing the river were a number of substantial houses (including the home of Nicholas Hawksmoor). By the 1680s Tufton Street had produced a crop of houses, indifferently built, on its eastern side, and Sir Robert Marsham was ready to let other land to builders. (The part of modern Marsham Street lying south of Horseferry Road was Grosvenor, not Marsham, property.) The proud stone name-tablet with its archaic spelling ('This is Marsham Stret, 1688') now inset in marble, survives near its original site on the Queen's

One of the most substantial properties in the area, with its own garden, meadows and tenements, was 'Dacre House, near Tuthill', bequeathed in 1595 by Anne, Lady Dacre, to her nephew, Robert Sackville, later Earl of Dorset. It was probably through the family of Sackville's wife, Lady Anne Clifford of Stirton, in Yorkshire, that the grounds of 'Sturton

49. Looking north from Horseferry Road along Marsham Street, 1925; pen and ink sketch by Hanslip Fletcher. The date on the King's Head pub is imaginative - the site was not developed till the 1760s.

50. Plan of the grounds of Peterborough House 'as they appeared between the years 1734 and 1748'. 'Market Street' is now part of Horseferry Road.

Head pub at the top of what was originally a cart-track to Bennet's hop yard.

Marsham Street was built up only slowly, one or two houses at a time; by 1720 it was a dead end reaching only half way to Horseferry Road, and the last ground north of Horseferry Road was developed first about 1767. The Earls of Romney, as the Marshams became, were financially crippled by gaming, royal entertaining, and grandiose reconstruction of their country house at Maidstone, and in the late 18th and early 19th centuries gratefully sold off property in Westminster when the price was right. Thus streets such as Medway Street and its neighbouring terrace on Horseferry Road were developed about 1812.

BUILDING ON MILLBANK

The Market Meadows, some eighteen acres lying south of the part of Horseferry Road formerly known as Market Street, passed after the death in 1662 of Hugh Audley, a rich court official, to his nephew Alexander Davies. In the three short years before his own death during the Great Plague, Davies began development of the river front, south of the horse ferry, with a line of houses. He also began building

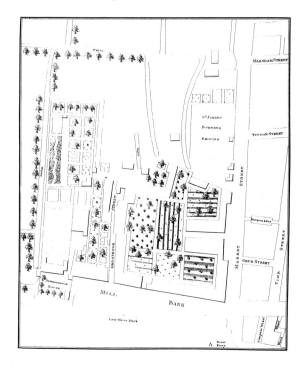

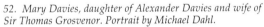

51. *'The House of the Earl Grosvenor on the Bankside Westminster', published by Robert Wilkinson in 1821. The mansion was taken down in 1809 to 'facilitate the great Improvements making in that neighbourhood'. The inset at the bottom shows the first house in 1666, built by Alexander Davies.*

52. *Mary Davies, daughter of Alexander Davies and wife of Sir Thomas Grosvenor. Portrait by Michael Dahl.*

himself a mansion at the end of this terrace, on part of the land now occupied by the Millbank Tower. Until the first decade of the 19th century, the carriageway on the riverbank ended at the forecourt of this great house, and between here and Chelsea was no more than a rutted and muddy footpath (illustration 31).

Davies's death left his affairs in a mess. By 1673 the Millbank mansion was in the occupation of the Earl of Peterborough, who later carried out substantial repairs and improvements, including pumping arrangements for draining water from the grounds. The situation of Peterborough House was described in 1720 as "but bleak in the winter, and not overhealthful, as being near the low meadows on the south and west parts."

In the meantime, Alexander Davies's infant daughter, Mary, had been married by her mother and stepfather to a young Cheshire landowner called Sir Thomas Grosvenor, as a means of rescuing the estate's finances. The unhappy heiress, whose father's financial crisis dominated her childhood, was pursued in her adulthood by illness and scandal; her

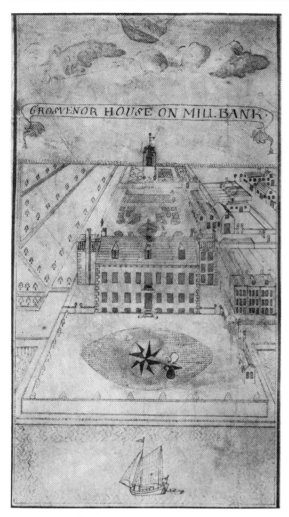

53. *Grosvenor (Peterborough) House on Millbank. It shows industrial development to the north-west of the grounds.*

54. *One of the Davies houses on Millbank, etched in 1894 by Rowland Paul.*

mental stability was uncertain, and as a young widow she was preyed upon by an unscrupulous priest, who had her secretly married to his brother. Mary Davies's Grosvenor heirs did not establish a home on Millbank until after 1732, when the house was extensively refitted and extended, and became known as Grosvenor, Belgrave or Millbank House. By this time there had been substantial rebuilding between the house and the ferry. Various industrial processes had been established on some of the leased ground. Next to the mansion the lessee established a distillery; a brewer and a sugar-baker also set up business nearby. The presence of thirsty travellers - and the dilatoriness for which the ferrymen were famous - accounts for the Davies development also including at least two pubs.

Though some of the early building survived until the early 20th century, Peterborough House was demolished about 1809 to make way for the road from Westminster to the new Millbank Penitentiary. By this time the riverside north of the ferry was described as "lined with rubbish, boats and old vessels". Page Street and Thorney Street were pushed westwards by Horseferry Road builders and stone merchants, businesses which thrived around the Millbank wharves. They included the substantial stone merchant, John Johnson, who made his fortune from London street improvements, and whose paviour's yard behind Horseferry Road accounts for the 19th-century sign of the Paviour's Arms.

55. *Queen Square, now Queen Anne's Gate, by T.H. Shepherd, 1850. Visible is the iron railing which separated Queen Square and Park Street, which are now merged into one thoroughfare. Queen Anne's statue may be seen by the first building which juts out on the right.*

Streets and Squares

QUEEN ANNE'S PRECINCT

The odd bulge midway down Queen Anne's Gate is explained by its being originally two separate streets, on two separate properties, and indeed (until 1873) separated by a low railed wall near the Queen's statue. Until the end of the 17th century the land was unbuilt on, and lay behind the medieval inns and houses in Tothill Street.

The broader, western end was Queen Square, which was built on a back plot belonging to an inn called the White Hart on what is now the north side of Broadway. The Square appears to have been built about 1704-5, by a speculative builder, by trade a goldsmith, called Charles Shales. Originally there were 24 houses and an Anglican chapel, all of which had by 1720 been acquired by Theodore Janssen, a director of the South Sea Company. Janssen lost his fortune in 1723, following the bursting of the 'South Sea Bubble'. It is extraordinary, given that it fell so early into more than a dozen different hands, that the Queen Square development has survived so intact.

The eastern end, originally known as Park Street, stands on land bequeathed to Christ's Hospital in 1554/5 by Richard Castell, a local shoemaker who had invested his earnings in property in Tothill Street and King Street. The streets to the south were opened up by the Earl of Dartmouth (in association with the notorious speculator Nicholas Barbon) and Sir Edward de Carteret, the lessee in the 1680s. Park Street was first developed at much the same time as Queen Square. At the same time, an old alley called Maiden Lane was developed by its owner, Thomas Sutton, and became what is now Old Queen Street.

The earliest houses in Park Street itself were, seemingly, less well built than those in Queen Square, and were "ruinous" by 1769. The street must then have seemed poor indeed by comparison with Great George Street, built up by a speculator, under authority of Parliament, and occupied from 1755. Park Street was thoroughly rebuilt over the next decade, partly by Christ's Hospital itself, partly on a building lease by another speculative builder. Certainly, ever since, it has been a solidly respectable address, and home among others to Jeremy Bentham, James and John Stuart Mill, and the infant Palmerston. Comparison of the western and eastern sections of the combined street demonstrate how, during the first half of the 18th century, town building had become more systematic and uniform: wooden eaves and

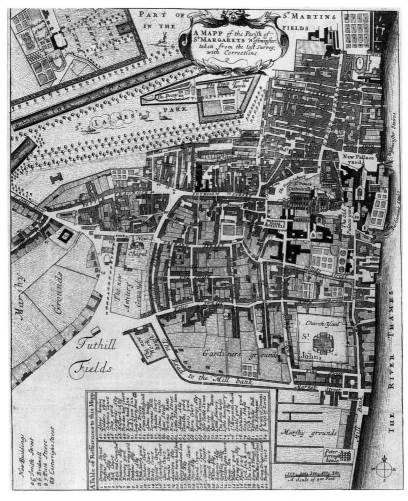

56. *St Margaret's parish, a map revised in 1720 on the basis of a survey of the 1680s by William Morgan.*

cornices were forced to disappear for the sake of fire prevention, window sashes were recessed to a minimum depth, and, at the same time, decorative features, if they appeared at all, became standardised. There were no more grotesque animated keystones such as enliven and distinguish the houses of Queen Square.

A STILL PLACE

Between Horseferry Road and the Abbey, the property of Sir James Smyth (quite distinct, seemingly, from that of the Smiths of the Vine Garden) was developed around the end of the 17th century, with a turnpike at its northern end, and is now Great Smith Street. Towards the river, land acquired by Barton Booth, a successful actor, whose country residence was at Cowley, near Uxbridge, was built up as Barton, Cowley and part of Great College

Streets from 1722 A group of local building tradesmen each took several plots of land, being granted renewable thirty-one year leases of the houses they built.

By this time the population of St Margaret's parish was estimated at some 20,000, about a tenth of whom could be accommodated in the parish church or the Broadway chapel. The Church Building Commissioners therefore identified it as a prime candidate for one of their intended fifty new publicly-financed churches, and bought land between Tufton Street and Millbank from Henry Smith (as it happens, their Treasurer) for the new church of St John the Evangelist and an approach from Millbank. St John's was begun by 1713, but unforeseen difficulty with the subsoil meant that the church took 15 years to complete. By this time, Henry Smith's heir, another Henry, had found a building developer for what little land

57. St John's Church, Smith Square, in the mid-18th century. Gayfere Street (originally John Street) was built in the early 19th century, and renamed in 1909, after Thomas Gayfere, a local stonemason who worked on the restoration of Westminster Abbey in the early 1800s.

remained in the family, to the north of the church. This developer was a Millbank lime merchant called John Mackreth, who took charge in 1726 of the building of North Street (now Lord North Street) and the neighbouring sides of Smith Square and Church Street (Dean Stanley Street). Many of the builders of Barton and Cowley Streets, some of whose craft skills were also employed in building St John's and other Commissioners' churches, moved in to work for Mackreth, being granted 61-year leases of the houses in return. The remainder of the Square was developed later, and unsystematically.

Two novelists have given us their impressions of the surroundings of Smith Square. Dickens, in *Our Mutual Friend*, found here "a deadly kind of repose, more as though it had taken laudanum than fallen into a natural rest." And here, in what she described as "a still place", lived Sybil, Disraeli's symbol of the ordinary people, among streets "that had rather the appearance of streets in a very quiet country town, than of abodes in the greatest city in the world". Both writers emphasise the 19th century character of this neighbourhood as an artisan quarter. Barton and Cowley Streets (though far from being an artisan quarter) to this day convey the quality of stillness which in Smith Square was formerly so compelling.

VINCENT SQUARE

The Square was built up by 1813 on its two northern sides with solid semi-detached, cottage-style villas, on uniform plots but to a variety of designs, best exemplified by nos 3-4 and 84-5, though 7 and 8 must have followed soon after. Later, from 1863-70, bow-fronted terraces by Benjamin Hudson and John Reid made tighter use of the remaining available front-ages, including some side-land, and the last section to be built was between Bloomburg and Udall Streets, in 1882, replacing sheds and cottages fronting away from the Square. The names of these and neighbouring streets, like the Square itself, commemorate various local clerics, or Westminster headmasters. Though the square was thoroughly respectable, the area just to the east enjoyed an evil reputation. The school made no objection to the Westminster boys making full use of their good fortune in their extensive playing fields, but they were under orders as to the route they might choose to reach them. Regency Street and Maunsel Street were out of bounds; the approach had to be circuitous, by the north-west corner, from Rochester Row.

Perhaps the residents were only too relieved when, in 1846, the district police court moved here from

58. *The forge and veterinary premises run by Caroline Cooper in the 1880s and 1890s. The premises stood at the corner of Smith Square and the south side of Church Street (now Dean Stanley Street). Other premises on the south side of the Square included scrap-dealers' businesses and St John's Rectory.*

59. *The north-east side of Vincent Square in 1845, showing the Westminster scholars' cricket tent, a small audience and some uninterested sheep. Lithograph by Radclyffe.*

60. The Police Court in Vincent Square, from the Illustrated London News, *10 Jan 1846.*

cramped quarters in Queen Anne's Gate. New offices were built but the appearance of the premises suggests that a pair of the original semi's have survived in an adapted form. Police horse patrols have been mounted from this base, now extending into Rochester Row, since 1869.

The Square has consistently been attractive to institutions. The earliest was the Tothill Fields Trust, which was formed to deal with matters such as paving and lighting the new streets in the Fields, which lay beyond the jurisdiction of the parish vestries of St Margaret's and St John's. It first met at the Royal Oak nearby - since rebuilt. Shortly afterwards, in 1826, the Trust established itself in a double-fronted cottagey building on the site of the office block now numbered 1 Vincent Square. Since the arrival of the police, other institutions, several of them medical, have gnawed away almost all of the original Regency cottages.

Maunsel Street, the abode of 19th-century artisans and tradesmen, was developed on building leases, from 1823, by Paul Storr, a successful silversmith, on his father's market garden. Its chief curiosity is its name. Storr did not have foresight of the London County Council's abhorrence of overworked street names, confusing to all and in particular to fire

61. The meeting house of the Commissioners of the Tothill Fields Trust, at the corner of Fynes and Carey Streets. A sketch before demolition, 1856.

brigades. He, or his builders, allowed the thoroughfare to be known simply as New Street. In 1939, to the outrage of residents, the name was changed. The present name was chosen to commemorate John Mansell, a prebendary of St Paul's, who in 1256 gave an extravagant outdoor feast at his manor of Tothele. Alas, Tothele was Tottenhall, near the modern Euston, and nothing to do with Tothill Fields at all.

62. *Lambeth and Westminster from Millbank, By W. Parrott.*

Public Works and Private Enterprise

CROSSING THE RIVER

Until 1750, the only means of crossing the river between London Bridge and Fulham (other than in the exceptional winter when the Thames froze over) was by hired boat or public ferry. Proposals for a bridge to Lambeth had been made at least as early as 1670, but Parliamentary bills for a bridge were dogged by opposition from the City, which controlled London Bridge. Various alignments were mooted (Nicholas Hawksmoor proposed a bridge at the horse ferry itself), but in 1736 a Parliamentary committee selected a site at the Woolstaple, just north of New Palace Yard. With minor adjustment, it was here that the bridge was built, under the direction of Charles Labelye, a Swiss engineer. The project was troubled throughout. It was to be privately financed. All five of the lotteries promoted to finance the bridge failed to raise enough money, and in the end Parliament had to come to its financial rescue. Bad winters caused delay; and there was sabotage from aggrieved watermen. In 1747, just as Labelye had pronounced the works complete, several of the piers began to

W. PARROTT, DEL. ET LITH.

settle in to the river-bed, and the bridge was not finally ready for use until the end of 1750. The midnight celebrations involved trumpets, drums and cannon above, and French horns testing the echoes from sailing craft below. The crush of sightseers on the following day was such that many people had to hire boats home from Lambeth.

Until the opening of Westminster Bridge the famous Vauxhall gardens were typically reached by boat: wherries transported pleasure-seekers across by the coachload. Vauxhall Bridge, opened in 1816, and its necessary approach road, projected from 1811, stimulated the improvement of Millbank. This iron bridge was privately financed. The first two

engineers quarrelled with the directors; the iron bridge was begun by its designer, the second of the three, John Rennie, and finished in 1816 under the direction of Jeremy Bentham's brother, Samuel.

The stability of Westminster Bridge became suspect again when cracks appeared in 1759. In 1811 Rennie was called in and gave it a life of five to six years, though nothing was done and Thomas Telford, some twelve years later, was more optimistic. The old bridge survived, in ever-poorer condition, until the rebuilding of the Houses of Parliament. A design for its successor, built of iron, commissioned from Thomas Page in 1854, was in full use by 1862.

Though the first Westminster Bridge, which was

63. *The Vauxhall Bridge from Millbank, by T.H. Shepherd. It was replaced in 1906.*

64. *The New Bridge at Lambeth, from the* Illustrated London News, *22 Feb 1862. It was replaced in 1932.*

not only convenient but toll-free, had put an end to the horse ferry, it was still possible throughout the first part of the 19th century to hire a boat for long or short river journeys. Rules (similar to those for modern taxis) governed the way in which watermen could ply for hire and the fares they charged, and the number of recognised plying places seems in fact to have increased, between Westminster and Vauxhall, after 1800. In 1862 the Lambeth suspension bridge at the old Ferry place, projected at least since 1836, was finally opened, enabling foot passengers to cross for a half penny and a horse for twopence. The tolls on Lambeth and Vauxhall Bridges were abolished in 1879, after the bridges had been acquired by the Metropolitan Board of Works.

STREET IMPROVEMENTS

The Commissioners appointed to promote the first Westminster Bridge, under the leadership of the Earl of Pembroke, had also the task of improving the warren of medieval streets between the Palace of Westminster and St James's Park. King Street, in particular, was not only notoriously congested, but also poorly maintained, rutted and bumpy. A long-standing grievance of the King Street shopkeepers was the number of cabmen choking their doorways while plying for hire. Most significantly, as the enabling Act recited, this state of affairs was "prejudicial to commerce". The result, following a Hawksmoor proposal for a broad street all the way to Charing Cross, was Parliament Street, parallel with and east of King Street from Downing Street southwards. Nos. 2 and 3 survive from the 1750s. Eventually Whitehall itself was widened, and in 1759 the end of this phase of street improvements was signified by the removal of the so-called Holbein Gate of the former palace (illustration 11). Bridge Street, with new building leases granted for houses on both sides, was occupied only after building works ceased on the bridge itself. Great George Street (of which no. 11 survives) was a private speculation by one James Mallors, who obtained Parliamentary powers, the first houses being built by 1755.

The Commissioners were by statute required to ensure the modish "Beauty, Regularity and Uniformity" of the new street, and saw to it that certain trades - including the selling of fish - were excluded from the development. Surplus stone from the bridge was bought for a new fish-market, old market premises having been obliterated by Parliament Street. The fish-market was a failure - City interests working to starve it of supplies - but a meat market, on the present site of the Middlesex Guildhall, survived until the opening up, in the first decade of the 19th century, of the space that became Parliament Square.

65. A View of New Palace Yard, Westminster, by John Boydell, about 1750. The new houses on the extreme right lay back-to-back with others in Bridge Street

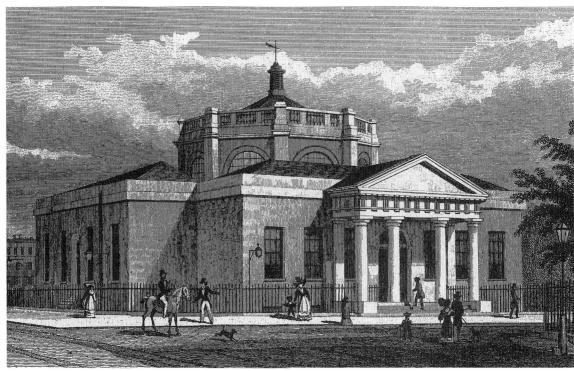

66. *The Middlesex Guildhall, built in 1805 and demolished in 1892. By T.H. Shepherd.*

67. *An early 19th century view of Parliament Square looking towards Old Palace Yard. An impromptu fight is in progress in the centre of the picture: the onlookers include the driver of a water cart.*

68. The main entrance to the Horseferry Road gas works. Lithograph from a drawing by the architect; Thomas Faulkner, c1845.

GAS COMES TO LONDON

The first years of the 19th century saw an innovation that within two decades was to transform cities: the manufacture of gas for lighting. Demonstrations in Soho and at the Lyceum theatre, and the patronage of the Prince of Wales for a birthday celebration at Carlton House Gardens, confirmed public interest. The end of the decade saw the establishment, under Parliamentary authority, of the Gas, Light and Coke Company. After an abortive beginning in Shoreditch, in 1812, the company acquired premises south of Great Peter Street - Providence Court, and Laundry Yard - for manufacturing gas, from coal shipped by barge to wharves on Millbank. Thus Westminster acquired the world's first functional gasworks. The inhabitants of Laundry Yard were treated to a private view of the new technology, but were subsequently terrified by the explosion which occurred when workmen lit a candle to explore the source of a suspicious smell. In 1814, when their Pall Mall offices came under threat of demolition, the company's board of directors took to meeting here as well.

In the autumn of 1813 the company began its first major public contracts, for lighting in St Margaret's parish and on Westminster Bridge. Though the inhabited parts of St Margaret's were lit by 1819, and expansion beyond the immediate area was rapid, the company's early years were not without setbacks, mostly attributable to the experimental nature of the technology. Shortly after public supply began, a gasometer exploded. Control of the dreadful smells produced by the manufacturing process was a constant problem, not completely solved even by 1849, when one Sunday in July the stench emptied the local churches in mid-service. The grand festival in the London parks to celebrate the temporary peace of 1814 brought the company the opportunity of demonstrating its prowess by lighting St James's Park for the event; when the specially-built pagoda (illustration 45) caught fire, the strange and alarming new process may have taken the blame in the public imagination, but the actual cause was the firework display. It was not long, however, before the company provided gas lighting in the Park as well. By 1837, it was supplying Buckingham Palace, and soon after that the new Houses of Parliament (which had their own special main, and special metering equipment in suitably Gothic style).

Gradually the works absorbed most of the land between the backs of the houses in Marsham Street and the frontages on Great Peter Street and the Horseferry Road. They greatly impressed the French socialist writer Flora Tristan, who described a visit there in her *London Journal* published in 1842. Though she admired the machines, the majesty and terror of the huge furnaces, and the vast iron structures of this "palace of industry", she was horrified at the general heat, stench, and dirt, and the appalling conditions in

69. The yard at the Chartered Gas works; from the Penny Magazine *Feb 1842.*

which the stokers worked, attempted to rest, and constantly hazarded (for seven or eight shillings a day) sudden death from an accident or gradual death from tuberculosis. The company had, unsurprisingly, a poor reputation for labour relations.

The site was never an ideal one for its purpose, being just too far from the river for convenient supply of fuel. When the company's vast new plant at Beckton opened, production slackened off. It ceased altogether in 1875, though the site remained in use for storage, and the office accommodation (in what had become the company's head office) was rebuilt in magnificent style, expanding across Monck Street before the site closed completely after nationalisation in 1948. Gas storage had ceased here in 1937, when the gasholders were demolished, and their substructure incorporated in capacious underground hideouts linked by tunnel to the wartime Whitehall defence system. Some of the office fittings survive at the North Thames Gas museum, at Bromley-by-Bow.

The GLCC, although the first and the largest supplier of gas to London, was far from having a monopoly. Aspects of the 'gas wars' of the middle years of the 19th century were fought out in Pimlico; as a result of competitive pricing there were wage cuts, and consequent strikes, at the Horseferry Road works. Pimlico had been staked out as its territory by the Imperial Gas Company, but (in return for the chance to compete with the GLCC elsewhere) this body handed the territory over to the corrupt and incompetent Equitable Gas Company, which built a substantial works south of Tachbrook Street - round the outfall of the King's Scholars' Pond Sewer - in 1831. After twenty years of bitter public crossfire a truce in the 1850s led to higher gas prices. The Equitable was absorbed by the GLCC in 1871, and the Pimlico works finally closed in 1901.

After the Fire

WHITEHALL'S PRIVATE HOUSES

After Whitehall Palace was finally destroyed in the conflagration of 1698, the land lay desolate. Twenty years later the north-eastern part of the precinct was still covered with heaps of rubbish. The land was needed for no obvious public purpose. Into this vacuum moved enterprising and wealthy citizens, peers and Parliamentarians. Harrington House in Craig's Court, north of Scotland Yard, (rebuilt in the 1930s as part of a telephone exchange) dates from about 1702. On the wreck of the palace itself, from 1717 until the 1770s, a new generation of similarly grand town mansions spread over the massive site where the Ministry of Defence now stands. Most of these houses faced westward, across the remains of the old Privy Garden (later rebuilt as Whitehall Gardens). The Banqueting House became the Chapel Royal, and remained a military chapel until the end of the 19th century.

The grandest of all the grand houses were Pembroke House and Montagu House. The earliest Pembroke House, designed by the prolific Palladian architect Colen Campbell, stood with its own watergate and

70. *Entrance to Pembroke House, Whitehall , looking west towards the Banqueting House (then a chapel) in 1813.*

71. *Looking south down Parliament Street, from the roof of the Banqueting House, as drawn by J.T. Smith in 1807. King Street runs parallel on the right.*

72. *Mar House, superseded by Richmond Terrace.*

stairs to the river, just south of the centre of Horse Guards Avenue. It was demolished by the heir of the Earl who had chaired the Bridge Commissioners, and a new and much-admired successor created in 1757 by William Chambers. The larger Montagu House, built by 1733 at the southern end of the Privy garden, survived till 1859. In the meantime Peter Burrell, Surveyor General of Crown Lands and fa-

ther of the first Lord Gwydyr, in 1770 built in place of some of "old ruinous sheds" next to the Chapel Royal and the Lottery Office, the house which became Gwydyr House.

At the south end of the garden lay the premises which before the Union of Parliaments in 1707 were the headquarters of the joint Secretaries for Scotland, the earls of Loudoun and Mar. Nearby, facing the river, was Richmond House, built about 1660 and long the residence of the Dukes of Richmond. In 1791 fire, once more the scourge of Whitehall, destroyed Richmond House, and this entire group of buildings was cleared. The early 1820s had already seen the filling up of the east side of Whitehall Gardens with new residences (among the occupants were Sir Robert Peel and, later, Disraeli). From 1825, further building leases were granted, for the eight fine houses which became Richmond Terrace.

GOVERNMENT MOVES IN

From this time private residents in Whitehall found themselves increasingly surrounded by Government. As the 18th century leases fell in, it became more difficult to get them renewed. Public offices were

73. *The Board of Trade building in Whitehall, 1814, part of the palace of Whitehall which escaped the fire.*

74. *The new Board of Trade buildings by Sir John Soane; aquatint by Thomas Shotter Boys, 1824.*

75. William Kent's Horse Guards

found in Whitehall Yard from 1803; Pembroke House was taken over for the Tithe Commissioners in 1851, and the Passport Office moved to Whitehall Gardens in 1863. It is all the more surprising that the Duke of Buccleuch was, in 1856, granted a fresh 99-year lease of Montagu House, enabling him to rebuild it as "a palatial residence in the French Renaissance style". But the process of de-privatising Whitehall was a gradual one. Richmond Terrace was in its earliest days home to Huskisson, the economist and minister most famous for being the first railway fatality; in the 1890s to H. M. Stanley, the journalist and traveller. From 1850, however, the Board of Health was ensconced in no. 8, and private homes here gradually dwindled, disappearing entirely only in 1939.

The same process inevitably occurred on the western side of Whitehall, which escaped the palace fire. North of the maze of courts and alleys between King Street and the Park, a development of the 1680s on Sir George Downing's land was in part rebuilt for Sir Robert Walpole during the provision of new Treasury buildings by William Kent in the 1730s. Throughout various reconstructions since, the surviving buildings at nos. 10 to 12 have afforded official residences for senior Ministers. North of Kent's Horse Guards, reconstructed from 1745, further official residences were the present no. 36 Whitehall, built 1732-3 as offices with dwelling above for the Paymaster General; and the Admiralty, where some seven senior sea lords were accommodated. Dover House, built for Sir Matthew Featherstonehaugh in 1755, was subsequently occupied, and successively renamed, by the Duke of York and Albany (for whom Henry Holland created the screening portico, and a charming circular hall), Lord Melbourne and Baron Dover. It was not until the comparatively late date of 1885 that officialdom, in the form of the Scottish Office, captured this private residence also.

Government had already taken over the south western stretch of King Street. Sir John Soane rebuilt the west side as Board of Trade offices in the 1820s, to such a limited brief that Sir Charles Barry was retained to reconstruct them in the 1840s. Between them, this block, Sir George Gilbert Scott's Home, Foreign and Commonwealth Offices to the north (the subject of celebrated architectural combat with

76. *Scott's new Government Offices from St James's Park; lithograph by J. O'Connor c1865.*

Palmerston) and the complementary turn of the century block to the south, gradually eliminated most of early and post-medieval Westminster between King Street and the Park.

But there was never a grand plan. Barry had been asked, after winning the competition to design the new Houses of Parliament, to produce additional designs for a concentration of rebuilt government accommodation in Whitehall. These were not pursued, however, and an initiative of the 1850s for comprehensive reconstruction came to nothing. Like the palaces before it, bureaucratic Whitehall just spread, until today its outposts have crept almost as far as Victoria Station.

77. *Downing Street 1827, by J.C. Buckler.*

THE PALACE OF WESTMINSTER

Henry VIII's abandonment of the ancient Palace had left it free to become a centre for government. Westminster Hall continued to house the courts of law, whose daily business was halted only when there was need for a state trial or a grand royal occasion, and the House of Lords sat, when Parliament was in session, in their traditional quarters. Edward VI granted the Commons, who had hitherto met in the Chapter House of the Abbey, the use of the chapel of St Stephen - a move instigated by the Abbey authorities, for whom the college of canons founded by Henry III to serve the royal chapel had been a constant cause of rivalry and distrust. By the end of the 17th century the chapel roof required to be replaced, and Sir Christopher Wren classicised its medieval Gothic while lowering the height of the debating chamber. The Unions with Scotland and subsequently Ireland meant that further alterations were needed, and the addition of Scots peers required the Lords to move into larger accommodation in what had in its days as a royal residence been the Court of Requests, where the King entertained petitions, and was later a banqueting chamber known as the White Hall. Both chambers suffered persistent ventilation problems which were never, it seems, satisfactorily resolved. During the 18th century there had been plans for comprehensive rebuilding, but little was achieved beyond the creation of official residences for the Speaker and clerks. The growth of legislative busi-

78. *'The Destruction of the Houses of Lords and Commons by Fire on the 16th October, 1834. Drawn on stone by William Heath, from a sketch taken by him by the light of the flames.'*

ness towards the end of the century required further enlargement, carried out by James Wyatt in a manner his successor, Sir John Soane, was not alone in finding shoddy, and using materials which Soane warned would not survive a fire. As well as adding new Committee rooms and a library, Soane rebuilt the law courts to the west of Westminster Hall in the early 1820s, employing a neo-classical design for the facade which so offended his paymasters he was

required immediately to Gothicise it. He rightly complained that the enlarged accommodation for the courts was still unequal to the demands to be made on it; as indeed it remained until new courts were opened, closer to lawyers' London, in the Strand in 1882.

On the eve of its destruction the palace was the product, therefore, of repeated and continual pressures for rebuilding and enlargement; merely a jum-

be retained. It was not to be. Throughout the daylight hours of 16th October 1834, two workmen were employed to feed the House of Lords stoves with wooden tally sticks. These had formerly been used in an obsolete system of tax-collection but by this time were clogging up space needed for a new bankruptcy court. The flues caught fire. Despite the best efforts of the London Fire Office, the police, three regiments of guards and hundreds of individual volunteers (including the Prime Minister, Lord Melbourne), the ancient palace was, by the following morning, a smouldering ruin, though a seemingly miraculous change in the wind during the night had saved Westminster Hall.

Enough survived for the Commons to move temporarily into the Court of Requests, and the Lords to sit in the Painted Chamber - originally the King's bedchamber - while the architectural competition for the New Palace of Westminster, to be either Gothic or 'Elizabethan', was fought out. The remains of St Stephen's chapel were cleared away only when found to be too dangerous to retain.

The competition's clear winner, from a field of ninety seven, was Charles Barry, though disappointed rivals soured his victory by challenging the conduct of the judges. Barry's splendid conception, on a plan which was to be considerably modified in execution during the two decades of building, was enhanced both as submitted and as built by myriad detailed drawings, by A.W.N. Pugin, for Gothic furnishings of all descriptions. Tensions in their working relationship, and in years of frustration, as the designs were developed, with Parliamentarians and ministers were to lead after the death of both men to public dispute between their respective heirs as to the true authorship of the design; a dispute which seems sad and gratuitous in an age when architecture is more often than not recognised as the collaborative product of a fusion of skills.

ble of rooms on several different levels. The work of James Wyatt had destroyed many medieval murals; others were rediscovered in the course of the Soane alterations.

In 1833 a select committee of the newly-reformed Commons took evidence from more than a dozen architects. All but one recommended comprehensive re-building, though without dissent they insisted that the medieval beauty of St Stephen's chapel must

79. *Part of the response to the 'Fenian outrages'. 'The Police learning the cutlass exercise at the Wellington Barracks', from the* Illustrated London News *in 1867.*

'THE YARD'

The 18th century parish watchmen, with their rattles, staves and ill-maintained smoke-blackened lanterns, were notoriously ineffective. The twelve shilling weekly wage paid by St John's to its elderly watchmen was usually all that stood between them and the workhouse, and the St John's watch were typical of the London parishes of their day. The long campaign to improve the quality of London's policing eventually bore fruit, outside the City of London, in the Metropolitan Police Act of 1829, promoted by Sir Robert Peel as Home Secretary in Wellington's administration. The first two Commissioners, Colonel Rowan and Sir Richard Mayne, were greatly exercised by the necessity to raise the quality, and literacy, of the recruits who came forward. Their task was not made easier by the hostility of a press and public deeply suspicious of an institution which they took to be un-English, and to threaten state interference in traditional liberties (the press called the new police "the Duke of Wellington's gendarmerie".) Peel had foreseen the problem, and indeed the dark blue uniform and civilian-style headgear had been devised to look as un-military as possible.

The Metropolitan Police Office, charged for a brief

to their station by the men of the Whitehall section who entered and left the premises by Scotland Yard came by the 1860s to be adopted as the standard name for the office as a whole, even by those who had business with the senior officials whose domain was reached from Whitehall Place. While Scotland Yard remained the metropolitan headquarters, the Central, or Whitehall division of the uniformed force became 'A' division, the most prestigious posting in the force, with its main police station later established in King Street, then, from 1890, in Cannon Row.

The detective branch was founded in 1842, its expertise becoming such that from the 1860s provincial forces began to 'call in the Yard' when presented with a problem beyond their own resources. Illustration 79 demonstrates one mode of response adopted to a novel problem which presented itself from 1867, when Fenian activists began a bombing campaign which reached London, and Clerkenwell, in March, leading to a substantial increase in the force. A renewed campaign, beginning in 1883, brought bombs into Whitehall itself, causing substantial damage to Government buildings in the King Charles Street area. The underground railway line between Westminster and Charing Cross was blown up, though damage to Westminster Hall from another bomb was averted, and (in Westminster at least) there was no loss of life. The police response was to establish a section specialising in countering terrorism, originally known as the Special Irish Branch, a name from which the 'Irish' was later dropped.

The most audacious bomb was planted, in 1884, in the Scotland Yard headquarters themselves. This drew attention to the inadequacy of accommodation, in what the press described as "a dingy collection of mean buildings", for the administration of a force which had numbered 2,000 in 1829 but had since grown more than seven-fold. Fortunately for the Commissioners a site near Westminster Bridge, part of which was land reclaimed during the Embankment works of the 1860s, had been taken for a grandiose project to build a National Opera House, which despite a somewhat operatic launching ceremony in 1875 had swiftly run out of money. On the foundations of the projected opera house rose Richard Norman Shaw's New Scotland Yard. Opened in 1890, the first New Scotland Yard was already so inadequate for the needs it served that within a few years an auxiliary block was added on its southern side. In recent years the place-name 'Scotland Yard' has moved again, this time when the Metropolitan Police moved their headquarters to a new office block near St James's Park station. The old premises by the Embankment are now called Norman Shaw Buildings.

initial period with the policing of the Westminster parishes only, was set up in Whitehall Place. This was a street of modest speculatively-built houses inserted, in 1820, between Great Scotland Yard and Middle Scotland Yard, and used thereafter for the mix of official and residential purposes typical of the place and the time. No. 4, which had briefly been the headquarters of the Inspector-General of Cavalry, fell conveniently vacant in 1829, and the premises were altered so that what had been servants' quarters became the first 'station-house', with a new entrance at the back into Great Scotland Yard. The name given

Paupers, Prisoners and Patients

PALMER'S VILLAGE

Before this century provision for the poor was made in one of two ways: by taxing the occupation of property, or by private charitable gift. In Westminster, as on the City of London's eastern fringe, there was a substantial concentration of privately-founded almshouses for the aged poor, most of them around Palmer Street and the site of the Army and Navy.

There were royal precedents. Henry VII had founded almshouses outside the Abbey gatehouse, his mother in the Almonry just to the south west, and Henry VIII in the Woolstaple. Of these nothing remains. Of the foundation of Cornelius van Dun, of Brabant, who in 1577 endowed almshouses in Petty France and St Ermin's Hill, each for eight women, only the name of Vandon Street survives. Next was Anne, Lady Dacre, whose Emanuel Hospital was endowed on her death in 1595. In 1602 four acres on the edge of Tothill Fields, now the site of the St James's Court hotel, were purchased for a new building, the surplus land towards Palace Street producing a rental income from market gardening. There

was provision for ten men and ten women, most of whom were to be chosen from among parishioners of St Margaret's. One place each was reserved for nominees of the parishes of Chelsea and Hayes in Middlesex, where her ladyship had owned substantial estates. It would be an error to suppose that this foundation was administered for the most distressed and vulnerable: although no-one might be given a place if he or she owned more than £100 worth of goods, or £5 annually in land, anyone who was so physically or mentally impaired as to be unable to attend daily service in the Hospital chapel was to be required to leave.

The founder had also apparently intended that poor children should find a place in her hospital, by each almsperson taking in and bringing up an orphan. This combination of age and youth did not work, and it was more than a century before her ladyship's wishes were implemented in the form of the Brown Coat School.

Emanuel Hospital survived the building of Victoria Street only to reach the end of its life in 1894, when there were only eight inmates in the Hospital. By that time the building had come to be regarded as one of the most charming examples of its type in London. Strenuous local effort failed to save it, and the type is now best represented by the Trinity almshouses in Mile End Road.

Van Dun's and Lady Dacre's examples were followed through the 17th century by other local ben-

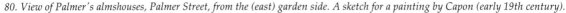

80. View of Palmer's almshouses, Palmer Street, from the (east) garden side. A sketch for a painting by Capon (early 19th century).

81. Van Dun's Almshouses, 1820. From Old and New London.

82. Emanuel Hospital (Lady Dacre's almshouses), 1887. Watercolour by E. Angell Roberts.

83. The rear of Emanuel Hospital, 1892. Watercolour by Rose Barton.

efactors, some on the Dacre model of a foundation intended both for the very old and the very young. One which covered the span of the generations was the foundation of the Revd James Palmer, the anti-episcopal vicar of St Bride's, Fleet Street. His Hospital, also known as the Black Coat School, housed twelve elderly men and women and twenty local boys, to all of whom Palmer himself ministered as chaplain. As he was described as 'a pious man and a painfull Preacher', the 'comfortable sermon' he regularly gave in the hospital strikes modern ears as a mixed blessing, but he was presumably only painstaking.

Palmer's foundation in what is now Palmer Street was, by the beginning of the 18th century, joined to the west of Buckingham Gate by a group of smaller institutions - Nicholas Butler's almshouse for 'two of the most ancient couples of the best report' (1677); George Whicher's for six aged men (1680) and Judith Kifford's (1705) for 'two decayed virtuous gentlewomen'. This group gave its name to the district: Palmer's Village.

Somewhat apart were the almshouses of Mr Emery Hill, a property speculator and dignitary of the Brewers' Company, who three years before his death in 1677 set aside funds for a group of almshouses, built on the north-west side of Rochester Row in 1708. Hill's intention appears to have been to mirror, but exceed, the munificence of Palmer. Instead of single men and women, he provided for six married couples and six widows; his schoolmaster was to have a

84. Rochester Row in 1840 showing Emery Hill's almshouses. By T.H. Shepherd.

higher salary; and the children were to have the additional benefit of being taught Latin. This attempt at competitive benefaction so over-reached the funds allotted that it was impossible to implement it fully until 1817.

It was on the Rochester Row site that all these foundations were ultimately consolidated, as the United Westminster Charities, in the present buildings of 1882.

POORHOUSE AND PRISON

There appears to have been a drive to systematise the administration of the poor law in St Margaret's in the first twenty years of the 17th century, when the population was expanding rapidly. This period saw the establishment of the bridewell, or house of correction for 'rogues vagabonds and sturdy beggars', which stood close to what is now the south side of Howick Place. Next to it was St Margaret's Hospital for poor children, also known as the Green Coat School. By mid-century the bridewell was also a county prison. An inscription from its entrance, built into the west face of the Middlesex Guildhall behind Parliament Square, says:

'Here are several Sorts of work
For the *poor* of this *parish* of St *Margarets Westminster*
As also the *county*, according to law, and for such as will
Beg and Live Idle in this City and Liberty of *Westminster*

Anno 1655'

A new workhouse was established 'in the Fields' by voluntary subscription of the parishioners by 1664. A commentator of 1705 noted drily that the 'Designe' for setting the parish poor to work 'in a short time became ineffectuall', and the building became first a lodging house, then was taken over for the Grey Coat Hospital. Ultimately a new poorhouse was established, first at the top of Great Smith Street, and later, when the site was absorbed into Victoria Street, at the south-west end of Petty France.

Intended to restrain and deter such as were seen as 'loose and disorderly persons', who were put to beating hemp, the Tothill Fields bridewell also served the parishes of St Martin in the Fields and St Clement Danes. By the beginning of the 18th century it had become a gaol for convicted criminals as well as a

85. The old Tothill Fields Bridewell, with a view of the courtyard and garden enclosed by security barriers.

means of detaining vagrants, and in 1776 the demolition of the Abbey Gatehouse prison added to the pressure on its space and led to its enlargement. John Howard had described it as remarkably well managed (by a private contractor). It had nevertheless a very restricted site, and its replacement, a county prison with 800 places for convicted criminals, remanded prisoners and debtors, opened in 1834 to the west, on the site of cowsheds acquired from a farmer called Francis Wilcox.

The massive granite portals of the prison were entered from the new Francis Street. From the distance of Piccadilly, according to an account of 1850, the bulk of the prison was readily mistaken for an outlying wing of Buckingham Palace. The inner precinct consisted of 'a spacious and beautifully trimmed garden, nearly as large as the shrubbery of Belgrave Square, but adorned with finer trees, and kept in better order'. For all the civilising influence that this suggests, no trades were taught or practised in the prison. Remand prisoners were subjected to the appalling 'separate' system, being isolated from all contact with fellow inmates. For the rest, the only activity available apart from oakum picking, which was expected to be carried out in silence, was the treadwheel. An exemption from this dreadful regime was made for any prisoner whose income was sufficient to provide for his maintenance; thus it was that a single inmate was noted by a visitor to be

spending his days studying Greek and mathematics. In 1850 the prison was set aside exclusively for women and boys under 17, and the regime was gradually modified.

86 & 87. Plan of the new Tothill Fields Bridewell and a front elevation view by T.H. Shepherd.

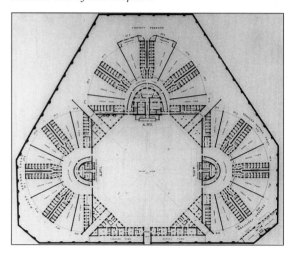

88. Boys exercising in the yard of the new Tothill Fields Bridewell.

89. Jeremy Bentham (1748-1832). Drawing by G.F. Watts

THE MILLBANK PENITENTIARY

The rebuilt Tothill Fields prison had a relatively short life; in 1877, when it closed, the remaining inmates were transferred to Millbank.

The prison on Millbank was vast and intimidating, and the site had been chosen partly for its isolation. It covered some 16 acres, 11 of which were gardens. Jeremy Bentham promoted a scheme (devised by his soldier brother Samuel) he described as a 'panopticon'. As conceived, this would have been a 'glass lantern', with the prisoners housed around its circumference. The revolutionary aspect of the concept was not only supervisory; the whole purpose of the institution, following the ideas of John Howard, was reform. The prison was an experiment, the only one of its kind in the country, and unique in being managed by central government.

From the very beginning there was trouble. Bentham spent a vast sum of money, and some twelve years of negotiating, designing and re-designing, moving his operations from Battersea to

90. Millbank Penitentiary, 1829.

Millbank in the process, without there being a prison to show for it. Only when taken over by the Government was the prolonged and expensive business of sinking foundations in the peaty soil finally conquered; and the design had been substantially altered, emerging as six pentagonal structures radiating from the governor's house, and surrounded by a vast perimeter wall with lookout towers. The first prisoners, a pathetic group of three dozen women brought in chains from Newgate, arrived in 1816, just as cracks were beginning to appear in the outer walls, signalling the need for massive rebuilding.

In 1823 the prisoners had to be evacuated because of an outbreak of disease. It was popularly supposed that the low-lying land was the cause, but in fact the disease was scurvy, and its cause a restriction on the prisoners' diet following a political fuss about its earlier, superior quality. This was followed by severe problems of discipline, leading to the introduction of the 'separate system', which itself led to numerous breakdowns and suicides. Then came the disastrous governorship of the curiously-named Revd Alexander Nihil, who set impossibly high standards for behaviour of both prisoners and staff, placing intolerable strains on both. By 1843 it was apparent that the reformatory experiment had failed, and Millbank

90. A female prisoner in the Millbank Penitentiary.

91. The shoemakers' workshop in the London Reformatory Institution, a voluntary body which provided work for male ex-prisoners in Great Smith Street in the 1850s.

became an assessment centre for candidates for transportation, although in the 1860s with the decline and eventual abandonment of this practice, further experiments took place here, including penal servitude, separate confinement and forced labour. Millbank ended its unhappy days as a women's prison, closing in 1890.

92. *The Samaritan seal of the first Westminster Hospital, based on Hogarth's mural at St Bartholomew's Hospital.*

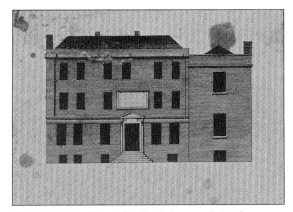

93. *Westminster Hospital in Castle Lane, as depicted on a certificate of attendance in 1830.*

THE WESTMINSTER HOSPITALS

The famous Westminster Hospital traced its origins to a 'charitable society', the first of its kind in London. In 1715 four gentlemen meeting in a Fleet Street coffee house founded a society which at first engaged in assisting the 'industrious sick and needy' on an out-relief basis. In 1720 a house in Petty France was acquired for in-patients. As with the other hospital foundations of the 18th century, patronage was the essence of the system, a 2-guinea subscription buying the right to nominate an in-patient and an out-patient at any one time. The founders' motivation seems in part to have been religious, for the 'reclamation of the souls of the sick' was pursued as well as medical care. On their recovery beneficiaries were expected formally to return thanks for the bounty of the Society.

The demand for medical services was such that almost immediately it was decided that the service should be confined to St Margaret's parishioners. Some of the gentlemen in charge, however, began to find this geographically, and perhaps socially, inconvenient. A faction who would have preferred to establish permanent premises north of the Park instead of accepting an offer, by the brewer William Greene, of a house on the corner of Castle Lane, took themselves off in 1735, and established St George's Hospital in Lanesborough House at Hyde Park Corner.

After almost a century in Castle Lane (on the present site of the Westminster Chapel), the Hospital spent its second century in Broad Sanctuary, where the Inwoods designed it a building in a Gothic style

intended to reflect its proximity to the Abbey. There was room here for more than 100 patients, but only two baths. The building was drained into a cesspool, until by the 1870s this could no longer be tolerated. A few years into its third century, the Hospital moved to its last site at St John's Gardens in 1939, when the Millbank area was being substantially rebuilt.

Also designed to assist the poor was the Western Dispensary, established in Charles Street in 1789, moving ultimately to 38 Rochester Row. Until it was absorbed into the National Health system, it latterly offered a nursing service, based in Bessborough Gardens, to patients in their own homes. The area round Rochester Row and Vincent Square area consistently attracted hospitals, beginning with three military hospitals: the Grenadier Guards, on the north side of the Row from 1801, the Coldstream Guards, in Vincent Square from 1814, and later the Scots Fusiliers, in Vauxhall Bridge Road. The Grosvenor Hospital for Women and Children grew in 1870 out of a voluntary dispensary in Vincent Square, and the Gordon Hospital (named after the general on his death at Khartoum) was founded in the Vauxhall Bridge Road in 1884, partly to conduct research into diseases of the rectum. The Children's Hospital, also designed to further research, into infant mortality, transferred from Hampstead in 1907 as a memorial to the late wife of one of its founders, Sir Robert Mond. The original Empire Hospital for Paying Patients, however, on Vincent Square and Vane Street, has become a hotel, the references to paying patients formerly embossed on stone entablatures being pointlessly obliterated in the process.

94. *Broad Sanctuary, showing Westminster Hospital. An undated photograph. In the foreground is the monument commemorating Westminster scholars killed in the Crimea.*

'Mr Cubitt's District'

THE NEAT HOUSES

Until Vauxhall Bridge Road was created, about 1815, the area between the riverbank and the few terraces around Buckingham House and the road to Chelsea was given over almost entirely to horticulture. In the area just east of the Chelsea water works, white lead works and Smith's distillery were established on what had been parkland anciently called 'the baileywick of Neate'. South of the Cross Road (now part of Lupus Street), as a by-product of the new road, tea gardens were laid out under the name of New Ranelagh, on what was formerly meadow. Otherwise, the whole area was given over to market gardens - easily the largest single area for vegetable produce so close, on the north side of the river, to the built up areas of London and Westminster.

Beyond the New Ranelagh gardens, in 1807 Hunter and Bramah had established steelworks, to which the only road was a track now traced by the line of Denbigh Street. They dug a large dock - the Belgrave Dock - across the garden ground lying between the tea gardens and Smith's distillery to the west. The distillery, and the older white lead works at the foot of Turpentine Lane, were reached by narrow lanes from the old wooden bridge across the inlet of the Chelsea water works at the Neat Houses, where Ebury Bridge now crosses the former basin of the Grosvenor Canal. The road to the distillery, originally Baker's Lane, became Distillery Lane and later, as to its northern stretch, Sutherland Street. The former road to the lead-works remains Turpentine Lane.

The whole area was part of the parish of St George Hanover Square. The lead works were on the property of a Mr Sloane Stanley, and the corridor where the Vauxhall Bridge Road was built belonged to the Wise family, as did the fields round Warwick Way. The new road generated new, and on the whole poor, building (like Garden Street on the former land of Wise the royal gardener). But most of what became the modern Pimlico belonged to the Earls Grosvenor, the heirs of Mary Davies, who had so little thought of housing development that in 1807 Hunter and Bramah were given a lease until 1873. Ten years later this lease was bought by John Johnson the stone merchant, but his strategy for redevelopment achieved just Thames Parade (from 105 Grosvenor Road to the William IV, and almost certainly sub-contracted) and a row of (more characteristically) indifferent houses, now long gone, running south from Lupus

95. Chelsea Water Works and the Thames, looking towards Westminster. From an engraving by J. Boydell, 1758.

96. Thomas Cubitt

Street. By 1825, frustrated by continued obstruction from the market gardeners he intended to dispossess, Johnson sold the remainder of the lease to Thomas Cubitt.

'SOUTH BELGRAVIA'

Considered as an enterprise, the sheer scale of the undertaking which Cubitt began, in Belgravia and what became the modern Pimlico, is nothing less than staggering. Little wonder that Pimlico became (to the palpable irritation of Grosvenor estate officials) thought of as 'Mr Cubitt's district'.

Fashionable London began, for the first time, to take a serious interest in the district then known as Pimlico when George IV, on the throne in his own right at last, began in 1821 to remodel the former Buckingham House. Until that point building in Pimlico was viewed as extremely insalubrious, and the tentacles of building that crept around the head of the Chelsea reservoir and along the the Vauxhall Bridge Road did little to dispel this image. It was the endorsement of the area by George IV which was crucial to the reversal in Pimlico's fortunes, and Victoria's continuation of royal approval is marked

97. Buckingham House, built as the town house of John Sheffield,1st Duke of Buckingham, in 1754.

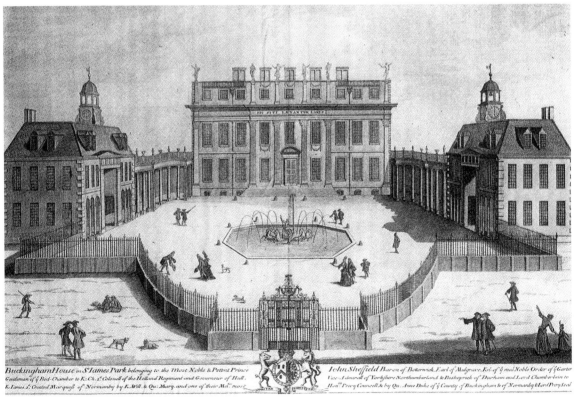

98 & 99. Thomas Cubitt's yard and works at Pimlico, c1845-50. The top view is looking west, the bottom illustration is looking east.

100. Victoria Square. Watercolour by Caroline Ediss, 1947.

by Matthew Wyatt's Victoria Square of 1838. In 1821 the Grosvenor estate, which had for nearly a decade been planning development around the King's Road to Chelsea, also finalised plans for laying out the Eaton Square area. Before long they also began transforming the old reservoir of the Chelsea water works into the Grosvenor Canal, an expensive business which never quite paid its way commercially, but nonetheless greatly assisted building operations.

In 1824, Thomas Cubitt secured what remained of available building land in an area called the Five Fields, by then coming to be known as Belgravia, between the King's Road and Belgrave Square. He was also about to undertake building on the Lowndes estate, off Knightsbridge. He was already a substantial builder - probably the most substantial in London, with developments completed on the Calthorpe estate off Gray's Inn Road, and under way not only in Bloomsbury, Islington and Stoke Newington, but also near his home at Clapham. In the following year, having divested himself, on advantageous terms, of a large tract of land north of the Canal, he not only staked out the land south of 'Cross Road' (Lupus Street) he had acquired from Johnson, but also obtained rights to 24 acres around Vauxhall Bridge Road from the Revd Henry Wise, and other land from Sloane Stanley. Thus he was able to plan road

101. The Grosvenor Canal; watercolour.

layouts as advantageous as the site would allow, with the minimum of artificial restraint imposed by estate boundaries. The names of the new streets reflect landownership: Hugh Lupus, first Duke of Westminster, married into the family of the Duke of Sutherland, and owned land at Eccleston in Cheshire. There was Wise property in Warwick, and in or near the Warwickshire villages of Tachbrook, Moreton and Lillington, as well as at Charlwood in Surrey. Cambridge Street was originally Kenilworth Street, and Alderney Street began as Stanley Street.

The Neathouse project was highly speculative, and took half a century to complete. The ultimate achievement was an extraordinary feat both of imagination and determination. Given the scale of the plan and the length of time necessary to achieve it, the financial commitment required, in a notoriously perilous industry, was enormous. Apart from the embanked road which ended on the riverbank at Bramah's old works, the only major route across the low lying and marshy gardens was the old Willow Walk, north of which lay reed-beds. The Vauxhall Bridge Road led to the new bridge, opened in 1816, and to a handful of shoddily built and minimally drained streets to the east, around Regent (Regency) Street. To the south of these, a developer called Hamlet who had proposed building on such of the Crown land as was not required for the Penitentiary had come gravely unstuck; Cubitt eventually added this land to his al-

ready extensive terrier. The level of the land was raised in 1827-8 by the spreading of soil excavated from St Katharine's Dock near the Tower of London and from elsewhere. Not least in importance were the covering in of the King's Scholars' Pond Sewer - forming the line of Tachbrook Street - at Cubitt's expense in 1844, and the Thames Embankment, approved by Parliament in 1846 but subject to so many delays by property-owners that Cubitt ran out of patience and built more than a quarter of it himself.

In 1839 Cubitt established an eleven-acre factory area on the river bank, on the present site of Dolphin Square. Here the joinery, glass, plasterwork, steel and marble, as well as some of the bricks and cement for the various building operations were produced, using the latest steam-driven technology, enabling the business in Pimlico and beyond to benefit from the sheer scale of production as well as control of the entire process. This concentration of workshops made the business singularly vulnerable to disaster, which struck in August 1854. Huge damage was inflicted by an outbreak of fire which took almost a full day to extinguish, and swept away the older part of the works, which had not been constructed of fireproof materials.

Cubitt had to clear most of the older gardening businesses out of the area in order to make the roads, but himself sub-let again for gardening, until he was ready to sponsor building on a large scale in 1840.

102. The Flask Tavern in Ebury Square; watercolour by J.P. Emslie, 1888.

The roads were formed in an ingenious combination of grids and diagonals, making best use of the space between ancient, and unchangeable, rights of way. Other than in respect of some of the grander houses, in Eccleston and Warwick Squares, and, later, St George's Square, Cubitt acted not as builder but as developer, agreeing with small-scale builders to sub-lease the land on satisfactory completion of the building of a handful of houses, or sometimes a whole block. Usually the first building to be completed on any of these sub-developments would be a pub. Cubitt retained the right to approve the designs, or provide them from his own expert drawing office, and subsequent use of the property was tightly controlled by restrictive covenants. The builders found houses on the side-streets easier to let than on the two main roads. Though by 1860 there was very little land lying fallow in Pimlico, such of it as was unbuilt on lay either around Cubitt's own vast works, or at the extreme ends of St George's Drive and Belgrave Road. Building land was not exhausted in Pimlico until some twenty years after Cubitt's death in 1855.

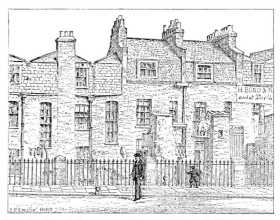

103. Tachbrook Street - rear of houses in Vauxhall Bridge Road. Etching in The Illustrated Topographical Record of London, 1898.

104. *Ebury Square; pen and wash sketch by Marjorie Croft, 1930.*

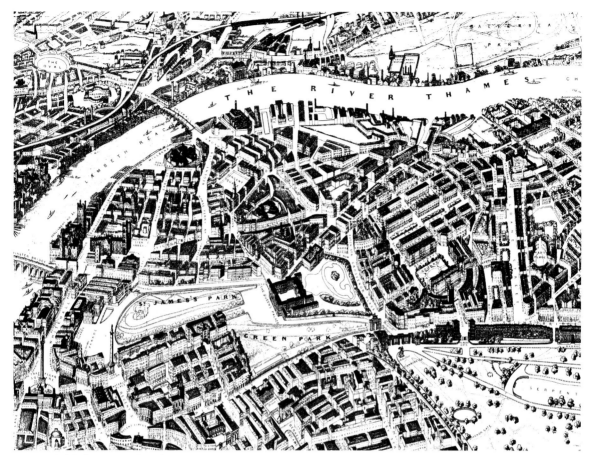

105. Banks's balloon view of London in 1851; section containing Pimlico.

AN ABODE OF GENTILITY

Even if, like Lady Alexandrina in Trollope's *Small House at Allington*, the fashionable could not contemplate life south of Eccleston Square, Pimlico beyond this limit had become, according to a contemporary description, an 'abode of gentility'. If they were not 'the cream of the cream', its residents were rentiers, artists, music or language teachers, or those with interests in the City. They would have 'a servant or two in the kitchen, birds in the windows, with flowers in boxes, pianos and the latest fashions of course.' (Indeed, artists, musicians and writers can be identified: Cambridge Street boasted Aubrey Beardsley, James Thomson lived at several addresses in Tachbrook Street and its immediate neighbourhood, and Sir Arthur Sullivan in Lupus Street.) The district was well supplied with churches and public houses, and in 1861 saw the foundation of the Pimlico Literary Institution (next to the Monster tavern which was now at the north-western corner of Winchester Street)

to afford its inhabitants 'rational amusement and improvement of the mind'. It was not only genteel, but comfortable; Cubitt prided himself as early as the 1820s that all his houses were equipped with water closets, and he was among the earliest builders to provide bathrooms in relatively modest houses. There is evidence, however, that different estate management policies by the Grosvenor and Wise landowners produced different standards of maintenance in later years.

It is a little sad, therefore, that the seedier side of Pimlico life is better recorded. As early as 1852, Henry Mayhew noted that the neighbourhood of St George's Drive was 'a district... prolific in loose women'. In particular, he identified this neighbourhood as one where an affluent man might seek a discreet introduction to the sort of 'quiet lady whose secrecy he can rely upon... who in all probability does not reside at any great distance; perhaps in

106. 'The Residence of the Revd James Hammond, Upper Belgrave Place'; lithograph published by the architect, H.E. Kendall, c1845. This house stood amongst the builders' yards of what is now the east side of Buckingham Palace Road, with the Grosvenor Canal basin (and later the railway) behind.

[Alderney] Street or Winchester Street, which streets everybody knows are ... inhabited by beauty that ridicules decorum'.

This reputation - to which, Mayhew hinted, proximity to Parliament was no disadvantage - clung to the district. Eventually St George's vestry established a committee to suppress the numerous brothels operating between Sutherland Street, Lupus Street and Tachbrook Street. They appear to have had some success, although the social researcher, Charles Booth, in 1902, could still describe the area between the station and Lupus Street as 'singularly unsatisfactory... swarming with prostitutes'. He found however that they usually roomed in pairs and made 'satisfactory lodgers', not as a rule taking their business home with them, but instead using small hotels in Vauxhall Bridge Road. By the end of the first decade of this century police action meant that passers-by were safer from soliciting, although round the station the unwary traveller might still find himself accosted by one of what the journalist George Sims described as the 'low class of unfortunates who come from Great Peter Street, Laundry Yard and the black area that lies in the very shadow of the Houses of Parliament'. In the neighbourhood of the station the authorities were not assisted by the fact that jurisdiction inside the station precinct belonged to the railway police alone, enabling the streetwalker to dodge inside one of the seven entrances, and avoid the grasp of the Met.

The Original Slum

THE DEVIL'S ACRE

In the mid-18th century the streets of Westminster were notoriously ill-paved and ill-maintained. Although repeated efforts were made to improve the state of the paving, lighting and street-cleaning in St Margaret's and St John's, nothing much could be done about the houses themselves. The worst area was acknowledged to centre on Old Pye Street, St Ann Street and Duck Lane (St Matthew Street). Here much of the property was owned by local charities, who were at the time inhibited by legal considerations from radical redevelopment.

Building here had never been on the grand scale, and gradually the gardens and courtyards with which the older houses had been equipped came themselves to be built over by increasingly unpretentious

107. Old Pye Street, drawn by Gustav Doré, c1870. The gables of Rochester Buildings are on the right; in the middle distance is the Catholic Apostolic chapel formerly at the corner of Old Pye Street and Abbey Orchard Street.

108. Duck Lane; pencil and wash by T.C. Dibdin, 1851.

dwellings, often without even an apology for drainage, and sometimes with no street access other than through the original premises. Though at the beginning of the 18th century Abbey Orchard street was new and considered well-built, Great Peter Street was described as 'of no great account', and Strutton Ground, which then extended further north than it does today, as 'a good handsome long well built and inhabited street'. But Pye Street and St Ann Street, ominously, were considered 'better built than inhabited'. It was not long before these streets and Duck Lane came to notoriety as the core of an area which was characterised not only by poverty and misery of a degree that today we associate with the third world, but by criminality such that an investigating clergyman was warned in 1846 that he was risking his life.

It was Cardinal Wiseman, writing of this area, to whom is attributed the popularisation of the word 'slum' in its modern sense. In a tract of 1850 he described the 'congealed labyrinths of lanes and courts, of alleys and slums' in the neighbourhood of Westminster Abbey. Dickens, more bluntly, called this the Devil's Acre.

Under Parliamentary powers obtained in 1845, Victoria Street was cut through the Almonry, Dacre Street, and the northern ends of Duck Lane and Strutton Ground. The slums, however, did not go away. Indeed the vicar of St John's estimated that the work displaced five thousand of the poor from their homes. Although three quarters of these left the district, mostly crossing the river to other poor districts, the remainder crowded into the courts and cottages that were left, living three or four families to a house built for one. A local missionary estimated in 1855 that in one of the area's 24 common lodging houses an average occupancy might be one hundred and twenty people a night. 72 lived in one of the twelve six-roomed houses in one court. From another, in the course of three months, 69 young people had been sentenced to transportation, and one hanged at Newgate. Half the population were, it was estimated, burglars, pickpockets, forgers or prostitutes; the other half, beggars and hucksters. Another clergyman found that more than nine in every ten Westminster beggars (he counted more than 800) were quartered here.

Such a famous slum in the City's heart was bound to attract the efforts of well-meaning and well-to-do social improvers. A ragged school was set up in Old Pye Street, in a house where the local Fagin formerly gave practical lessons in 'fobology', or the art of the pickpocket. A group of ladies, under the patronage of the Countess of Shaftesbury, employed a paid social worker to visit the women of the area in their homes, and through a series of 'mothers' tea meetings' and the distribution of tracts endeavoured to save the souls of the fallen or endangered, as well as

109. Great Peter Street, from the corner of Perkins' Rents, looking east towards St Matthew's church. Pen and wash sketch by T.C.Dibdin, 1851.

Great Peter Street Westminster T C D 1851

offering practical help in the form of needlework training, or occasionally money or clothing. In 1856, the Westminster Female Refuge was founded for prostitutes willing to reform; this survived until 1903 in the comparative tranquillity of Great College Street. A Miss Adeline Cooper was the guiding genius of another enterprise, which, from beginnings as a working men's club in Duck Lane, with its own provident societies, cricket club and library, went on to establish a lodging house maintained to what was, for the area, an unaccustomed standard of cleanliness. This was so successful that in 1866 it moved to a larger site on the corner of Abbey Orchard Street and St Ann Street, where not only accommodation but a lecture and reading room and a co-operative shop were provided. In its turn, this paragon of lodging houses disappeared when the site was appropriated for a rehousing scheme.

The same fate befell Westminster Chambers, converted in 1851 from three 17th-century houses by a Mr Reading, and regarded as one of the better examples of a type of which the area was not short. Here some 250 men could buy a night's accommodation and the use of a communal kitchen for between fourpence and sixpence each.

The most enduring of all the voluntary institutions founded in the area began in 1866, at the instigation of a group of architectural students. St Andrew's Club for Boys is believed to be the oldest club of its kind in the country, offering educational and sporting activities for boys and accommodation for those in work. Moving to Soho five years after its foundation, it returned to Great Peter Street in 1884, and is now in Old Pye Street.

MODEL DWELLINGS FOR FAMILIES

From the late 1840s - when Victoria Street was taking shape on the ground - a number of voluntary organisations were established, with the aim of proving that it was possible for the minor capitalist to invest in projects to build decent and affordable housing for artisans, and at the same time to produce a respectable rate of return on the investment - what came to be known as 'five per cent philanthropy'.

Most of the 'model dwellings' movement's buildings took the form of blocks of flats, then a form of housing in its infancy in England. The first block in Westminster was built in 1862 in Old Pye Street, on

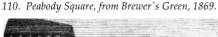

110. *Peabody Square, from Brewer's Green, 1869.*

111. Buildings erected by the Improved Industrial Dwellings Company at Semley Place and Ebury Square. Shown here are Ebury Buildings and Grosvenor Hall (Club).

the corner of Perkin's Rents, by a City merchant called William Gibbs, who named them Rochester Buildings. They still stand - the earliest block of flats of this scale surviving in London to be built by a private individual. Their distinctive Dutch-style gables rise above the hovels in Doré's sketch (illustration 107) as a graphic prospectus of what was possible 'before' and 'after' deliberate housing improvement. In 1877 Gibbs's widow sold the buildings to the Peabody Trust. Though they pre-date the Trust's own first development in Spitalfields, they were designed by the same architect, Henry Darbishire, and share a distinct family resemblance.

George Peabody, an American banker who had settled in England, funded London housing to the extent of half a million pounds. Building all over London in the 1860s, in 1868 Peabody came to Westminster in the form of Peabody Square (illustration 110), later Chandos House, which disappeared in post-war development. Here, on the site of Whicher's and Kifford's almshouses and bounded by Palmer Street and Brewer's Green, east of the Bluecoat School, were three blocks containing 93 flats (and the trustees' board room). Typically, the flats shared laundry and sanitary facilities, but the provision of fireplaces in some of the bedrooms made them a little less austere than the average. The flats were only available to families earning around twenty to twenty three shillings a week, and demand was said well to exceed supply. Even so, the trustees were criticised for out-pricing the poorest among those whom the buildings displaced from their homes (and for the crimson cloth curtains that appeared when the guinea-a-week tenant 'got on' in the world). There was a resident superintendent, who acted as rent-collector, but the tenants were claimed to be 'subject to no unnecessary restraint or supervision'.

Clearance of the slums produced flats for artisans' families such as the original inhabitants of Duck Lane could never have afforded. When in 1877 on the recommendation of the local medical officer of health the Metropolitan Board of Works secured Parliamentary approval for a scheme to clear and replace accommodation for 1,380 people in and near Old Pye Street, it was the Peabody trustees who redeveloped

the site, creating the Abbey Orchard Street and Old Pye Street estate, followed by a smaller development between Rochester Buildings and Great Peter Street. The first blocks on the Peabody estate in Pimlico, built on surplus railway land (formerly Sloane Stanley property), were opened in 1876.

As the Peabody Trust was forging its strategy, the City stationer, Sir Sydney Waterlow (and MP for Westminster), himself founded a company, the Improved Industrial Dwellings Company, aimed at what he called the 'wage-earning classes'. His builder, Matthew Allen, devised distinctive flats with balconies, graced by cast-iron railings, leading from a staircase which wound spirally down the centre of each block. Coburg Buildings (1875) (now called Coburg Close) in Greencoat Place were, before extension in 1986, completely typical. Others, now demolished, stood in Upper Garden Street and Ebury Square. Coleshill and Lumley Flats (1871-5) in Pimlico Road, like Ebury Buildings, benefited from land made available on less than an economic rent by the Marquis of Westminster. Here some atypical decorative features have blossomed. Though the IIDC was careful as to the creditworthiness and behaviour of its tenants it did not confine itself exclusively to a working class tenancy: in its flats just over the border into Chelsea, at the foot of Chelsea Bridge Road, middle-class residents were to be found in the blocks with a river view, artisans in the 'artisan blocks' behind.

In 1871 the original pioneers of 'five per cent philanthropy', the Metropolitan Association for Improving the Dwellings of the Industrious Classes, built Gatliff Buildings (named after their first secretary) amongst the sawmills in Ebury Bridge Road.

Amongst employers, only the brewing industry tended to feel the need to provide good cheap housing for its workers, because of the early start draymen had to make on their deliveries. Castle Buildings in Palace Street, built in 1883 for Watney employees at the Stag brewery opposite, were another of the many imitators of the 'improved industrial dwellings' of Waterlow - whose statue stands, coincidentally, in the forecourt of the Westminster City School almost next door.

Church and Mission

CHURCH AND CHAPEL

The plague of 1625 drew attention to the need for more burial space, and in St Margaret's the early years of the century had seen much new building. The Dean and Chapter granted land at the north end of Tothill Fields, and a bequest of 1631 from one George Darell led to the building of the Broadway Chapel, opened in 1642. This modest but evidently attractive classical building, one of the earliest English churches conceived as a Protestant place of worship, stood to the north west of the burial ground, which survives as the patch of open space at the angle of Broadway and Victoria Street.

'QUEEN ANNE'S FOOTSTOOL'

Though the Broadway Chapel, as it came to be known, was claimed to seat well over a thousand, within a century the parishioners of St Margaret's could have filled both churches ten times over. Thus the parish came to be amongst the earliest to benefit from the Act of 1710 under which up to fifty new churches were to be built in suitable parts of London.

An acre of land was available at the unbuilt, south end of Marsham Street, and another on Henry Smith's

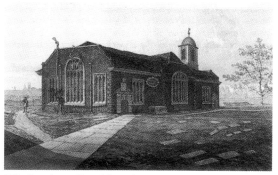

*112. Broadway Chapel from the north-east, by
R.B. Schnebbelie, 1817.*

property near Millbank. The latter was chosen (it was the more suitable site, but it is curious that Smith was treasurer to the Commissioners). Building was in hand by 1715 on the new church of St John the Evangelist, which was formally constituted a parish church in 1724. Like much other building in the area, it ran into difficulty because of the nature of the soil - part sank during building, requiring alterations in the design (including the much-abused towers, which were added for support). Opened for worship in 1728, the church had to be rebuilt, with Treasury assistance, after a disastrous fire in 1742.

The Church Building Commissioners always aimed for the splendid. What is now thought to be Thomas

113. St John's, Smith Square. View across the Millbank wharves from the river. An aquatint by T.H. Shepherd, 1815.

114. *Charlotte Chapel, 'near the King's new Palace, with the Sunday and daily schools adjoining'.Lithograph by C. Burton, c1830.*

Archer's masterpiece has consistently produced mixed reactions. The 18th century found it over-ornamented or 'whimsical', the 19th 'architecture gone mad'. Dickens was himself a little whimsical: it resembled, he suggests in *Our Mutual Friend*, 'some petrified monster, frightful and gigantic, on its back with its legs in the air'; the building's most usual nickname became 'Queen Anne's footstool'. Almost alone in support, Bohn's *Pictorial Handbook of London*, alluding to a gibe by Peter Cunningham, objected that if St John's can be criticised for looking like an upset parlour table, St Paul's merely resembles an inverted basin, and Gothic spires fire extinguishers.

Beside the many worthy clergy of St John's, who include Augustus Toplady, author of *Rock of Ages*, the most remarkable was a man totally unsuited to the profession in which he found himself: the satirical poet, rake and political journalist Charles Churchill, himself the son of a St John's curate. Able to publish sermons profitably on the reputation of his verse, Churchill abandoned his wife for a series of mistresses. His apparently voluntary resignation of his living in 1763 must have been received with relief.

In 1731 St John's acquired ground in Horseferry Road for burials (the vaults were unavailable for legal reasons, so were used successively as housing for the homeless, a carpenter's shop, and storage for a local brewer). Within twenty years the ground was full. Its level was three times raised to allow further interments, and the area extended in 1823, some thirty years before its final closure. A local campaign resulted, in 1880, in the Metropolitan Board of Works

taking the burial ground over. Turning it into a garden, they rescued it from long neglect.

As ever, the annals of scandal, crime and disaster are lengthier than those of serenity and success. Thus it is that not only is more known about Churchill than more sober-living incumbents; but more about precautions (largely successful) against grave-robbing than about the thousands of funerals, many spectacularly torch-lit, which took place here in the 18th century.

In similar vein, the proprietary Charlotte Chapel in Palace Street, built in 1766 by Dr William Dodd (now the core of the Westminster Theatre), is otherwise most memorable because of the fate of its founder, whose ambition led him into financial difficulties, and to forgery, for which he was ultimately hanged.

THE VICTORIAN CHURCHES

Churches were essential to marketing respectable suburban residences. As the 19th century saw building spread over Tothill Fields and the Neat Houses, church building had to keep pace.

War damage, a declining resident population, redundancy and demolition have been the fate of several of the Westminster churches, among them the Broadway chapel, rebuilt in the early 1840s as Christ Church, and St Andrew's, Ashley Place, built in 1855 to serve the development south of Victoria Street. The earliest of the Victorian wave was St Mary the Virgin, of 1837, in Vincent Square. It was designed by Edward Blore (who also completed Nash's

115. Christ Church, Broadway. Lithograph by T. Bury c1850.

MISSION WORK

Cundy was also the architect of St Barnabas, off Pimlico Road. Unlike his other churches, which had predominantly middle-class congregations, St Barnabas was designed to carry a High Church presence into the heart of a poor district. The inspiration of W. J. E. Bennett of St Paul Knightsbridge, the richly-furnished church adjoined a collegiate precinct which housed the school, the choristers and the church's four priests. This was a time when practices such as lighting altar candles or the wearing of certain vestments raised deep and widespread passions, and in 1850, only months after becoming vicar, Bennett became the focus for popular anti-ritualist sentiment. On one occasion, in a scene which prefigured worse and more persistent thuggery in East London later in the decade, the police had to be summoned to prevent a crowd screaming against popery from breaking down the church doors during a service. Bennett — criticised by Lord Shaftesbury and opposed by his bishop — resigned, and left London, though St Barnabas remained a beacon of Anglo-Catholic worship.

Other churches founded to take the Anglican message into poor areas were G. E. Street's St James the Less, of 1861 ('a Lily among weeds' of the Garden Street area, said the press) and St Matthew's, Great Peter Street, designed by Sir George Gilbert Scott to have a spire for which the money was never forthcoming. From its consecration in 1851 the stoical clergy and worshippers of St Matthew's had to face the audible hostility of the neighbourhood, expressed in the form of breaking glass, beating empty barrels under the windows during service, and on one occasion a savage assault on a scripture reader. Steadily, mission work in the area produced clubs, a penny bank, loan societies, reading and refreshment rooms, literacy classes, practical training in trades and cookery, and the falling off of the overt opposition of the slum.

Which is not to say that the missionaries' achievements matched their aims. Writing fifty years after these initiatives began, Charles Booth and his team researching the *Life and Labour of the London Poor* found that, despite enormous effort and expense, as well as attractive services and often exquisite music, the churches did not attract the poor. Nor did the various Anglican or non-denominational mission rooms designed to take a more user-friendly religion closer to their everyday lives. In a thinly-disguised description of St Matthew's parish, Booth recounts that a youths' institute had died with its foundress, a men's club perished after three successive secretaries stole its funds, and the ragged school had been superseded by the Board school. Apart from a block of lodging houses - presumably Miss Cooper's - only

reconstruction of Buckingham Palace) on the initiative of John Jennings, rector of St John's. It was followed by the much more elaborate St Stephen's, in Rochester Row, endowed by Angela Burdett-Coutts. After the First World War, it became apparent that the area could not support both churches, and St Mary's was pulled down in 1923 as redundant.

Modern Pimlico had been assigned (with the heartland of the Grosvenor estate in Mayfair) to St George Hanover Square when that parish was created out of St Martin in the Fields in 1725. Landowning interests were eager to foster respectable middle-class colonisation, and thus St Gabriel's in Warwick Square was built on Grosvenor land in 1853. Thomas Cubitt provided the ground in Bessborough Gardens for Holy Trinity, and his executors for St Saviour's in St George's Square and All Saints, Grosvenor Road — the latter at first a temporary iron structure. St Gabriel's and St Saviour's, like St Michael's in Chester Square, were designed by Thomas Cundy, surveyor (as had been his father) to the Grosvenor estate. Holy Trinity, and the later St Philip's in Buckingham Palace Road, were demolished in 1955, and All Saints in 1974.

116. *All Saints, Grosvenor Road. An iron church, c1865. To the left is Thames Parade, the legacy of John Johnson's early lease on Thames bank (see page 72).*

117. *Tea Meeting for the mothers at the 'One Tun' Ragged School, Old Pye Street, in 1858.*

118. *St James the Less. From* The Builder *15 June 1861.*

of fund-raising by his successors, was opened for worship in 1903. The Cathedral, designed by J.F. Bentley, stands on the site of the Tothill Fields Bridewell.

Protestant dissent has offered a formidable capacity in the area from the middle of the 19th century. An important Methodist presence was established in 1849 with the foundation of their training college (later run as a teacher training college by the London County Council) in Horseferry Road, a great gloomy building on the site of the new Channel 4 headquarters, near an earlier Wesleyan chapel (the site of the modern Church of the Sacred Heart). There has been a Methodist chapel in Westmoreland Terrace from its earliest days. Central Hall, on a scale and a site reflecting the presence of the Abbey and the Cathedral, dates from 1911. A Baptist chapel in Romney Street was founded in 1805, and another stood just west of Watney's brewery. The congregation at the Westminster Chapel in Buckingham Gate, formerly the site of the Westminster Hospital, traces its origins to 1840, and the present chapel was built in 1865. With 2,500 seats, it was said to be amongst the largest in London, and second only to the famous Dr Spurgeon's Tabernacle at the Elephant and Castle.

119. *Westminster Cathedral, by Howard Penton.*

a Sunday school and a mothers' meeting remained of the earlier enterprise in this parish, where missionary effort continued to be seen as more needed than elsewhere. There were four separate mission initiatives in St Matthew's, two in St Margaret's and one in St John's.

DISSENTERS

Statistics gathered in 1706 suggest that St Margaret's then had, with fifteen acknowledged Roman Catholics, the highest number in any of the Westminster parishes. By 1767 there were some 75 in central St Margaret's and St John's. The first Roman Catholic place of worship here is said to have been established in Petty France (then York Street) in 1792, being abandoned after a few years for financial reasons. Services were run by the Neapolitan ambassador in Great Smith Street from 1802, and a temporary chapel established in Dartmouth Street. Finally the congregation came to rest in Horseferry Road, in St Mary's chapel, 'an unpretentious building' built in 1813 where the Baptist chapel now stands. (The landowner was Lord Romney, a staunch Anglican, and the sale suggests the depth of his financial difficulties.) A mission chapel, in Palace Street, became, in 1857, the chapel of St Peter and St Edward. Finally the Cathedral, projected since Cardinal Wiseman became the first Roman Catholic Archbishop of Westminster in 1850 and achieved through half a century

Road and Rail

HORSE POWER

Until the 1860s, the district depended largely on privately owned or privately hired horse power. The network of horse buses which had been established from the 1820s, taken over from various independent proprietors by the London and General Omnibus Company in 1855-6, merely skirted the fringe. In 1825, when large-scale development had barely begun even in Belgravia, a single coach plied between the neighbourhood of Buckingham Palace and the City, making three return journeys a day. Pimlico was at this time, by this yardstick, insignificant as a residential suburb, taking a fraction of the traffic going to Peckham, Kensington or Kingsland; it was nevertheless, by comparison, well supplied with private stabling. Though by 1840 there were thirty buses, owned by a dozen different proprietors, operating between Chelsea and the City, the opening up of the Westminster district to public transport was made difficult by the absence of a good through road, and awaited the building of Victoria Street. Things had improved round the Abbey, however, as the notoriously appalling surfaces in Parliament Street and Whitehall were macadamised by 1832.

Victoria Street was the scene of one of London's earliest tramway experiments when, in 1861, an American with the unexpected name of George Francis Train laid a single line of rail from Westminster Abbey part of the way along Victoria Street. Based on a prototype from his native Philadelphia, Train's tramline was raised above the level of the street and thus presented a hazard to traffic. He failed to gain support in Parliament for the extension of his idea, and it was some ten years later before horse trams became accepted in London.

THE MAIN LINES

In the 1830s the Great Western Railway had threatened to build its London terminus on the west side of Vauxhall Bridge Road, at the end of a line bisecting Thomas Cubitt's proposed development of the Neat Houses, and incurring his implacable opposition. The Great Western's revised plans settled for Paddington instead. A further abortive scheme proposed bringing the West End of London & Crystal Palace Railway a little nearer the West End than its so-called 'Pimlico' terminus at Battersea, terminating near Artillery Row.

Railways reached the area at last in 1860, when the Grosvenor railway bridge, the first over the Thames, opened for traffic. It carried the London Brighton & South Coast Railway across the river from its previous terminus at Battersea (shared with the Crystal Palace Railway), into Victoria station, completed in 1862. The lines north from the new bridge were laid along a drained part of the Grosvenor Canal, bought from the Duke of Westminster. Precautions taken, with limited success, to protect the amenity and

120. Horse buses in Whitehall early this century.

PARLIAMENT STREET.

121. George Train's experimental tram, which ran along Victoria Street, 1861. The scheme was not a success: apart from other criticisms, the rails were raised above road surface level and were therefore a hazard to other horse traffic.

value of the streets near the railway, included rubber-bedded railway tracks, long glass trainsheds, extensive shrubberies and a prohibition on access for goods trains.

The new route was shared with the London Chatham & Dover Railway, which in its turn co-operated with the Great Western, whose West London extension railway, bringing traffic from Southall, looped south through West Brompton and Chelsea to join the Chatham at Clapham. The western, 'Brighton' side of the new station was flanked by the magnificent French-looking Grosvenor Hotel, designed by James Knowles. The smaller 'Chatham' side, always the poor relation, nevertheless came by the end of the 1860s to be host to traffic from several other railway companies bringing passengers into London, in addition to the Great Western. The London & North Western came from Willesden through Kensington; others chose, or were obliged to choose, more circuitous routes. The Great Northern came from Barnet by way of Farringdon and Brixton; the Midland from Finchley Road by a similar route. By 1908 the sheer inconvenience of these round trips made these routes early casualties of electrification

of tram and tube, as well as the recently-introduced motor bus. The Willesden and Southall services ended after the First World War, leaving the station to the original south coast routes, and increasing traffic from Channel boat-trains. There was substantial re-construction in both the stations (more radically on the richer, Brighton side) in 1908.

MORE TRAINS AND TRAMS

Another Victoria station was opened in 1868, to take the Metropolitan District Railway being finished that year, as part of the 'inner circle'. In 1878 it was joined to the larger stations by means of a passenger tunnel. The building of this section of railway, between South Kensington and Westminster Bridge - said to have involved some two thousand workmen, two hundred horses and 58 engines - afforded the opportunity of further slum clearance, and the widening of Tothill Street, beyond what was strictly necessary for the making of the station called St James's Park. Trains ran initially between Westminster and South Kensington, but plans to continue the line in to the City were frustrated by financial and negotiating difficulties. The work was linked with the new Vic-

122. 'Arrival of the Workmen's Penny Train at the Victoria Station'. From The Illustrated London News, 1865. From the early 1860s, Parliament insisted that the railway companies provide cheap early-morning tickets from the suburbs.

123. *The construction of the Metropolitan Railway at Westminster. From* The Illustrated London News, *16 March, 1867.*

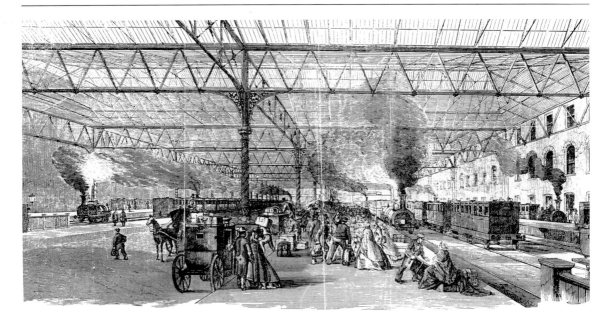

124. *'The new Victoria railway station at Pimlico'. The interior of Victoria Station, from* The Illustrated London News, *4 May 1861.*

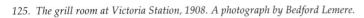

125. *The grill room at Victoria Station, 1908. A photograph by Bedford Lemere.*

126. *Victoria Station 1901, by Howard Penton.*

toria Embankment. A station in Cannon Street opened in 1871.

Trams were shortly to arrive in earnest; like the railways, they forged a route across the river. The Pimlico, Peckham, and Greenwich Street Tramways Company (soon merged into the London Tramways Company) established a route from Victoria Station across Vauxhall Bridge to Kennington in 1873, but the gradient over the bridge was thought to be too steep for the rails, and passengers travelled across the river in old-fashioned horse buses. Through tram-traffic had to wait for a new bridge - and electric trams - in 1906, the year in which trams (by then a London County Council monopoly) also first crossed Westminster Bridge on their way to Blackfriars. The tramways company never established the line it planned across Lambeth Bridge to Artillery Row. Nor did trams penetrate north of Victoria or south of Euston, a fact which contributed to the development, or lack of it, of amenities south of the Park.

Traders

VICTORIA STREET

It took the improvement-minded spirit of the 1840s - and a clearer focus on the horror of the slums - to bring to reality the need for a road link between the Abbey and the Palace which had been perceived as long before as the 1760s.

It was not at the top of the public agenda. Improvement Commissioners busy in New Oxford Street and Spitalfields were empowered by an Act of Parliament of 1841 to put aside money for the new street between the Abbey and the neighbourhood of the Palace. This did not happen - new streets did not make money; and in any event further legislation was required, in 1845, to set in train the purchases that had to precede demolition and reconstruction.

Work began at the Abbey end, though the houses in the middle stretch around the top of Strutton Ground were not obtained until 1849; the street was formally opened in 1851. This new street was no different from its predecessors, and clamouring builders did not beat a path to the Commissioners' door. For long enough, the Post Office treated it as if it was two streets, one by the Abbey, another extending north east from the terraces of Vauxhall Bridge Road which are now incorporated into Victoria Street at its western end. The gaps lasted longest in the middle, though there was some building here, notably Wood's

brewery on the corner of Artillery Row (1852). The Albert pub, now the only surviving building from the first generation of development in the street, was built about 1864. Contemporary was Vickers' distillery opposite (which became the Army and Navy Stores).

Victoria Street saw the first flats in London intended for middle-class occupants; it was however another twenty years and more before this French (and Scottish) manner of living captured the imagination of such Londoners as could afford to be choosy about their homes. A block on the street frontage itself opened in 1853. Nearby, the first of the six elegant blocks back-to-back in Carlisle Place and Morpeth Terrace, designed by Charles O. Parnell, date from 1859 and are the earliest surviving, of their type, in London. Grosvenor Gardens, from 1865, introduced the new concept of furnished apartments.

At the Abbey end, another first came in the shape of the 130-bedroom Westminster Palace Hotel, of 1861, on the Tothill Street junction. It was the first of its kind not associated with a railway, and to be provided with lifts. It also boasted ample space for business meetings, and separate 'gentlemen's and ladies' coffee rooms'. Several MPs made it their London residence. At the other end of the street were the Oriental Baths, a short-lived venture by a group of Irish speculators, opened in 1862 and intended to capitalise on a fad for Turkish baths then current in Dublin. Like the hotel, the Baths had separate facilities for men and for women, but, more unexpectedly, also offered special baths for horses.

127. Before Victoria Street - sketch from the Windsor Castle, Vauxhall Bridge Road; aquatint by W.A. Thompson, c1845. The Tothill Fields Bridewell is on the right of the picture.

128. The beginnings of Victoria Street, from the east with Westminster Hospital on the right. From The Illustrated London News, *6 Sept 1851.*

The mansion flats, chambers stuffed with professional consulting rooms and the head offices of railway companies and Parliamentary lobbyists, crept only slowly in to fill up the gaps. Westminster Palace Gardens and Artillery Mansions, blocks of the 1890s vastly more decorative than was typical of the street, were last to arrive and have thankfully not yet departed. Victoria Street took until the 1920s to acknowledge its potential for shopping, and only with post-war redevelopment has it fully unbent from its pose of Victorian upper-middle-class distaste for trade.

Retail premises were at first largely confined to the neighbourhood of Allington Street, and Victoria Buildings - the now-threatened block opposite Victoria Station where in 1872 Horace Overton first established his fishmonger's and game-dealer's business, later the still-thriving restaurant.

SHOPS AND MARKETS

For the most part retailing in Westminster has been a very local business, and the shops of the small, street-corner variety. Until the end of the 19th century Tothill Street was a bustle of such shops. Retailing in Rochester Row, Warwick Way and Marsham Street developed during the 19th century, turning residential frontages into an almost unbroken line of shop fronts. Pimlico's oldest family business, Wehrles the jewellers of Warwick Way, lasted from 1832 until very recently. The funeral directors, Kenyon's, at 74 Rochester Row, succeeded Whiteheads, established by 1876.

The largest family retailer, Frederick Gorringe's, originated in 1858 as a linen draper's, gradually spreading sideways along Buckingham Palace Road to become a fully-fledged department store. There

129. The beginnings of Victoria Street, from the west. From The Illustrated London News, *6 Sept 1851.*

130. The Oriental Baths in Victoria Street. From The Illustrated London News, *21 June 1862.*

131. *The Westminster Palace Hotel.* From The Illustrated London News, *25 Feb 1860. The architects, W. and A. Moseley, designed their 'monster hotel' after inspecting more than thirty hotels in continental Europe.*

132. *Windsor House in Victoria Street, 1954. It was built as the Army and Navy Hotel in 1881-3 to the design of F.T. Pilkington.*

being no dynasty of Gorringes, the business faltered in the 1960s, succumbed to takeover and closed.

The street markets have long been of great importance in the area. A small market in Chapter Street, where on Saturday evenings itinerant costermongers such as the orange-seller in illustration 137 came to dispose of their remaining wares, declined from its height in the 1850s to a mere handful of barrows by the end of the century; another small group traded from barrows in Lupus Street. The market now held in Tachbrook Street seems to have originated in a market of more than 60 stalls, mostly selling food-stuffs, which started in the mid-1860s in Warwick Way between Belgrave Road and Wilton Road. The other important market, in Strutton Ground, was believed in the 1890s to have been established some thirty years earlier, but it is clear from Shepherd's picture (illustration 133) of the corner of Old Pye Street and Duck Lane, a matter of yards away, that there was street trading in the area earlier than this. This market to this day maintains the balance between fresh foods and hardware that it manifested a hundred years ago, though it has shrunk somewhat and no longer spills out into Horseferry Road. At that time there was one old clothes stall in every five. The second-hand book stall has also vanished. The markets in Broadway - a 17th-century hay market, and a general market that scandalised the Sunday observance lobby of the 1850s - have each for their different reasons gone completely.

133. A fish stall at the corner of Duck Lane and Old Pye Street. Watercolour by T.H. Shepherd, c1850.

134. Wood block advert for the short-lived Abbey Shoe Mart, c1855, in a part of Tothill Street demolished in connection with the western end of Victoria Street.

135. A plea for funds from the Metropolitan Drinking Fountain and Cattle Trough Association, one of many such bodies which took advantage of the modest rents of Victoria Street and the nearness to Parliament.

NOTA BENE!
ABBEY
SHOE MART!
IS JUST OPENED,
35, TOTHILL STREET,
WESTMINSTER,
Where the largest Stock and great variety is always on hand.

NO SERVING ON SUNDAYS.

In yonder Abbey Heroes lie,
Who for their country dared to die;
Contended many a sanguine field,
And only to grim death would yield;
But he that fights and runs away,
May live to fight another day;
For he that in the battle's slain,
Will never rise to fight again;
And when the fight becomes a chase,
He wins the day who wins the race.
But runners oft their labour lose,
For want of *Easy Boots or Shoes*;
Here men of war, or men of peace,
May give their shoe-bound feet release,
Then go abroad and battles win,
Or stay at home and save their skin!

**Remember!—The ABBEY SHOE MART,
35, Tothill Street, Westminster.**

METROPOLITAN
Drinking Fountain & Cattle Trough
ASSOCIATION.
SUPPORTED ENTIRELY BY VOLUNTARY CONTRIBUTIONS.

Offices: Victoria House, 111, Victoria Street, Westminster, S.W.

President.—HIS GRACE THE DUKE OF WESTMINSTER, K.G.
Chairman of Committee and Treasurer.—JOSEPH FRY, ESQ.
Secretary.—M. W. MILTON.

THIS IS THE ONLY SOCIETY FOR PROVIDING
FREE SUPPLIES OF WATER FOR MAN AND BEAST
IN THE STREETS OF LONDON.

The relief it affords both to human beings and dumb animals is incalculable.

If it had not been for the operations of this Society, thousands of people, young and old, who now quench their thirst at the Fountains, would probably be driven to the public-house; and if it were not for the Troughs, the amount of suffering amongst the multitude of dumb animals continually crowding round them would be inconceivable.

Half an hour spent at one of them during the heat of the summer would do more to secure sympathy and support for the Association than any words which the Committee can use. They, therefore, very earnestly solicit liberal Contributions, and trust the work will not be permitted to languish for lack of funds.

136. *Early morning view of the shops in Princes Street, now Storey's Gate, c1865.*

137. *Orange stall in Grosvenor Road; watercolour by Ethel Wollmer, 1891.*

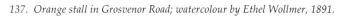

'THE STORES'

Any pre-eminence Victoria Street has today for retailing is owed, as it always has been, to one institution, which came there in the first place because the street's unfashionable character meant low rents. Now concealed under 'A & N', the logo bestowed on it since purchase in 1973 by the House of Fraser, the Army and Navy Stores opened in 1872 and provided a means of enabling serving or retired officers of the armed forces and their families, and serving non-commissioned officers, to benefit from bulk purchase and profit-sharing on the co-operative principle successfully promoted by the Civil Service Supply Association in the Haymarket. A modest beginning with a grocery department, in part of Vickers' distillery premises in Victoria Street, quickly followed by perfumery, drapery and tailoring, was so successful that shortly afterwards a gun department and carpenter's shop was added, banking and estate agency services provided, and a vast range of goods put on offer, from medical supplies, boats and wherries, to everything for the amateur taxidermist. In 1878 the Victoria Street premises expanded. At this stage a refreshment department was added, and shoppers who visited in person to avail themselves of the Society's prices could enjoy, despite 'irritating service', what the press described as London's best plain wholesome food at moderate prices; curry a speciality.

The retail trade was incensed by the Stores' success. A Parliamentary campaign against them eventually came to nothing; instead, stores such as Harrod's mimicked the competitive pricing policy. The Victoria Street premises were extended across a gangway to Howick Place. Further afield, branches were opened not only on the south coast, but in Leipzig and in India. By the end of the century there was criticism that the benefits offered by the stores were illusory, giving no serious advantage over conventional stores such as Harrod's, Whiteley's or the locality's own Gorringe's. Objection was taken that the profits were confined to shareholders, and not extended to subscribing members, and that the board members were overpaid.

In the 1890s the refusal of management to admit dogs to the premises, deputing staff to restrain them on the steps, caused some amusement in the press. Members who could not visit in person had access to a mail order service, by means of the weighty annual tome of which the catalogue consisted, and were expected to do so rather than send messengers to place their orders. An acrimonious press correspondence took place in 1876, when a member's messenger had been refused admittance to make a purchase as 'not a fit person to mingle in the crowd of members, including a large proportion of ladies'. Ostensibly concerned with the manner of the messenger's dress,

138. *The Army and Navy Stores dressed for 'Victory' in 1918. Before the plate-glass shop fronts of 1922, the building betrays its origins as industrial premises.*

the dispute was really about class, the Stores' management taking the line that the Society's members did not come there to mingle with 'carriers and costermongers'. They may have assumed correctly. Some middle-class women regarded the Stores as a kind of club, equivalent to their husbands' clubs on the other side of the Park.

From an early date the Stores had undertaken their own manufacturing, first on the premises and later in and around Ranelagh Road. By the end of the century they were under fire for their wage rates both for retailing and manufacturing staff, allegedly kept below 25 shillings, and employment practices such as imposing fines for petty errors and infringements of rules. During the 1914-18 war the Stores' profits climbed substantially, and wage rates rose, though not in pace with living costs. A strike in 1919, called after a meeting at Central Hall had voted overwhelmingly in favour, lasted all of two days before the management capitulated, and was regarded as a landmark victory by the shopworkers' union.

Between the wars membership became freely available to all, and in 1922 what had become a fiction was abolished altogether. A further step towards making the Stores look like just another shop was the installation, at the front of the building, of plate-glass windows. This change was celebrated in a puff by the novelist E. F. Benson, who praised the service and atmosphere of the stores as remaining wholly unchanged by the innovations, and described them as offering 'Utopian shopping'.

"Daily Mirror" Photograph.   **GIRL PICKETS ON DUTY OUTSIDE THE
PREMISES EARLY IN THE MORNING.**

139. *Another Victory celebration at the Army and Navy Stores, but this time to celebrate the triumph of staff over the management after a short strike in 1919.*

GENTLEMEN'S SHIRTS AND CUFFS.

Westminster.
Doz. pairs 12/0

Lord Lytton.
Doz. pairs 9/0

Army & Navy.
Doz. pairs 12/0

Royal.
Doz. pairs 12/0

Soft Fronted Shirts in Flannel, Oxford Mat or Zephyr.
For prices see page 829.

Perfect.
Doz. pairs 10/6

Grosvenor.
Doz. pairs 10/6

Times.
Doz. pairs 12/0

American.
Doz. pairs 10/0

Paris.
Round or Square.
Depth 4 in., to sew on shirt
Doz. pairs 7/0, 9/3 11/0

Linen Dress Front .... each 1/9

Stanley.
Doz. pairs 12/0

Gentlemen's Soft Double Collars.
Sizes, 14 to 17½ in.

White or Coloured
Oxford Mat each 0/10
Coloured Silk and
Wool ...... each 1/4
Coloured Cashmere
each 1/6

GENTLEMENS' SHIRTS AND PYJAMA SUITS.

A large selection of materials in all the latest designs, for making Gentlemen's Shirts, Pyjama Suits, &c.

Comprising Cream and Fancy Silks, Cashmere, Remino Flannels, Oxford Mat, French Cambrics, Zephyrs, and Viyella.

Gentlemen's Sleeping Suits in great variety.
For prices see page 829.

140. A page from the Army and Navy Stores catalogue of over 1300 pages in 1907.

Westminster at Work

Until it closed in 1959, the business with the longest pedigree in Westminster was the brewery after which Stag Place is named. The stag was the creature on the coat of arms of the Greene family, who had been brewers around the Sanctuary area since medieval times. By the 1630s John Greene owned a great deal of land in the area then coming to be known as Pimlico. His son William established a brewery at the west end of Cabbage Lane, about 1641. Cabbage Lane became Castle Lane, after a hostelry near its top. John Greene, William Greene's cousin and heir, expanded the business, buying pubs across a large tract of Westminster, Chelsea and Fulham. The last Greene to be associated with the brewery was Edward Burnaby Greene, who neglected pubs for poetry. Soon after his death in 1788 the business was sold to Moore, Elliot and Co., and the brewery rebuilt in 1796. By 1850 other partners had been absorbed and the firm's style transmuted to Watney & Co., until further amalgamation with two Holborn breweries, Combe's and Reid's, at the end of the century. Today,

the only reminders of the business are Castle Buildings in Palace Street and Castle Lane, built in 1883 in the 'improved industrial dwellings' style for the families of Watneys' workers; and the Stag itself, perpetuated not only in the name of the Stag Place development but as the corporate symbol of Watney Combe Reid, a trading name still in use despite several complex reorganisations.

A brewery and a sugar bakery were amongst the 17th-century development of what became the Grosvenor property on Millbank, south of the 17th-century wharves between the Palace of Westminster and the horse ferry. An abundant water supply favoured brewing in general - Thorne's Westminster brewery stood on the Page Street site of the Westminster Hospital Nurses' Home, and Wood's Artillery Brewery in the no-man's land that was early mid-Victoria Street. (Wood's, on the site of Artillery Mansions, was later absorbed by Watneys'.) What was good for brewing was good for distilling, as in Seager and Evans' Millbank premises, Vickers' in Victoria Street and Octavius Smith's Thames Bank distillery. Smith's long survived the neighbouring white lead works and Bramah's steel works (which had itself replaced a paper mill). After the mid-19th century opening up of the Thames Bank it too was lined with wharves. The massive Hovis flour mills beside Vauxhall Bridge moved there from Millbank about 1912.

141. A watercolour by R.B. Schnebbelie, 1817, showing the Stag Brewery of Elliot & Co., and Pimlico Lodge, the former family home of the Greenes.

142. *Workers at Octavius Smith's Distillery, Grosvenor Road, c1870.*

143. *Thorne's Westminster Brewery in Horseferry Road: a lithograph by Warren and Martin, c1850. The Brewery stood south west of the crossing of Marsham Street and Horseferry Road. Its well was re-discovered during construction works for the Westminster Hospital.*

Creeping west from the wharves north of the horse ferry, manufacturing also colonised the south side of Horseferry Road in the wake of the gasworks on the north side. John Johnson was something of a poor man's Cubitt: from this centre the tentacles of his business encompassed not only repairs to the crumbling Westminster Bridge and cottage building at the Neat Houses, but streets of small houses as distant as (inevitably) Johnson Street in Somers Town. Broadwood's, the piano makers, had their main factory opposite the gasworks from the time of its move from Soho in 1858 until their departure to Old Ford in 1902. In Esher Street, part of Johnson's development off Page Street, a Mr Tulloch established a mechanised marble works for products intended to bring Italian taste into the British home; by the 1860s there were two other marble yards nearby. There were also coach-building yards and ropemakers' premises. A similar mix of building and coach-building trades could be found along the canal side of what became Buckingham Palace Road. Coach-builders and iron-foundries were found in unexpected

places, such as Hooper's in Victoria Street, and Rowell's iron fencing manufactory at the skirts of the Abbey. Colt's, the small arms manufacturers, operated for a brief period in the 1850s in Bessborough Gardens.

The presence of Victoria Station encouraged the development of major warehousing businesses. Hudsons Place, behind the station, still bears the name of the furniture repository which began business here about 1875. Taylor's, who boasted the invention of something they called 'Taylor's improved system of removing furniture', were established for a century in Ranelagh Road, being taken over in the 1950s (after severe war damage) by a firm in Gillingham Street. Bishop's, in the area until very recently, started as a sideline to a greengrocer's in Elizabeth Street in 1854; by 1871, the founder. J. J. Bishop, had found better business for his horse and cart assisting house removals in the growing Pimlico. The firm's first large warehouse was in Hugh Street; others, purpose built in Ebury Street and Lupus Street, were destroyed during air-raids in 1941.

144. Wharves at Millbank, c1900.

145. Castle's Shipbreaking Company at Baltic Wharf, Grosvenor Road, north of Vauxhall Bridge.

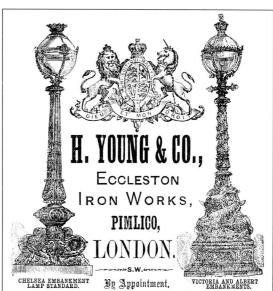

146. *Advertisement for H. Young & Co., of the Eccleston Iron Works, Eccleston Place, Pimlico.*

147. *The show room of the London Marble Working Company, Esher Street, Millbank, c1840.*

Government began to employ larger numbers, directly and indirectly. In 1857, it was decided to cut out private contractors in the provision of army clothing, to avoid profiteering, and an Army Clothing Depot was established in Bloomburg Street, later moving to a 7-acre precinct on the site of Cubitt's old yard, where Dolphin Square now stands. The premises, which were designed to provide a light and airy working environment, the antithesis of a sweatshop, employed more than 500 women (who had to be young, strong, respectable and childless) and 200 men. Nearby, the Army and Navy Stores had its own manufacturing premises, which expanded on moving to Ranelagh Road from Howick Place, and later expanded further.

But, since the establishment of Victoria Street and the encroachment of Government into Whitehall, this area has been increasingly characterised by office work - for which, ever since the coming of the trains, people have migrated daily into, and nightly out of, Westminster. The innumerable small offices and chambers of the early years of Victoria Street, the headquarters of railway and building companies, national charities and consulting engineers, established the trend towards clerical and administrative work which continues to characterise the area. Manufacturing declined. Between them, wartime bombs and post-war urban planning have gradually eliminated even the smaller industries such as printing, which survived, alongside brewing and milling, until the mid-twentieth century.

148 & 149. *Two scenes at Broadwood's Pianoforte Manufactory in 1858, from the* Illustrated London News. *The premises stood on the south side of Horseferry Road. Above, the view looks south to Page Street. Below, it looks north across Horseferry Road to St Matthew's Church in the distance.*

150. *The Royal Aquarium, Westminster, opened in 1876, now supplanted by the Central Methodist Hall. On the right is the Westminster Hospital, and on the left the Westminster Palace Hotel at the east end of Victoria Street.*

Amusements Rational and Diverting

MUSIC HALLS

The middle years of the 19th century saw a steady growth of music-hall entertainment in public houses. The Blue Anchor, on the south side of Petty France and the Three Jolly Gardeners (where there is now a car park) in Rochester Row offered music-hall in the 1850s. Similar were the Windsor Castle, and the Ship, on the north-western stretch of Victoria Street, which began life as part of Vauxhall Bridge Road, nearly opposite the main line station. Pimlico, though not renowned for this style of entertainment, had its own music hall, at the Queen's Arms in Warwick Way, on the corner of upper Tachbrook Street. This, like the Two Brewers in Buckingham Gate, gave up the music hall side of the business in the early 1880s, a period when the Metropolitan Board of Works was enforcing enhanced safety standards and many a theatrical management retired voluntarily. The Regent Music Hall, in a Regency Street pub on the

corner of Page Street, and not to be confused with the Regent Arms, closed by 1880, leaving the field clear in that quarter to the Westminster Temperance Hall, which lasted until 1886. The Temperance Hall was succeeded for three short years by the Victoria Theatre of Varieties in Marsham Street, which seems, on account of its alias as the Blue Ribbon Hall, also to have been associated with the 'taking the ribbon' arm of the temperance movement.

FISH, FOWL AND FLOWERS

Of more than merely local significance was the entertainment, in all its forms, offered at the so-called Royal Aquarium, opened in 1876 on a large site cleared for the laying of the District Railway at the north-east end of Tothill Street. Assuming a scientific pose which seems to have aimed to exploit the Victorian fascination with marine life, the edifying pull of the various fish-tanks must have been weaker than that of other kinds of entertainment on offer (which briefly included music under the direction of Sir Arthur Sullivan). On a day in November 1882, you could stroll through the winter garden on your way to visit an exhibition of sporting prints in the picture gallery, listen to a 14-piece orchestra from central Java, enjoy a lecture on opera or goggle at a programme consisting successively of gymnasts, con-

151. *The 'Rink Galop', as performed at the Royal Aquarium, Westminster. Aquatint music sheet.*

152. *The Royal Ornithological Society's cottage in St James's Park; lithograph by its architect, J.B. Watson.*

tortionists, vocalists and performing lions. Meanwhile, in the Annexe, Professor and Mrs Beckwith and their family of champion swimmers would demonstrate (no doubt with the utmost propriety) undressing, smoking, and eating two sponge cakes under water. When all this became too much, you could retire for billiards, repair for the latest newspapers to the reading room, patronise the smoking-gallery, or eat and drink in the grill room, the American Bar or the oyster buffet. Although those inclined to carp found all this 'third class entertainment for a third class public', there was nothing else quite like it in all of London.

Cultural aspirations were perhaps more convincingly met by a group of more specialised institutions. The Royal Ornithological Society established a headquarters in St James's Park in 1841 (illustration 152). The East India Company's museum collection was housed in Whitehall (illustration 154) before absorption into the South Kensington exhibition complex. The Architectural Museum, also ultimately swept into the Victoria and Albert Museum, had its origins in a museum and school of architecture established first in Cannon Row, then from 1869 in Tufton Street. It aimed to inspire working craftsmen as well as architectural students. The ancestor of the Army Museum took over the Banqueting House in Whitehall in 1890. And since 1904, the regular flower, fruit and vegetable displays of the Royal Horticultural Society have been a constant feature in Vincent Square. The Society marked their centenary in that year by opening the Old Hall as their permanent home, moving here from temporary premises in Buckingham Gate.

153. *The Architectural Museum, which stood near the northwest corner of Tufton Street, now the rear of Church House. It shared its premises with the Westminster School of Art.*

EDWARDIAN THEATRES

Despite its curiosities and delights the Aquarium was not a financial success. This was blamed variously on its being on the wrong side of the Park, and its being in central London at all when excursionists

154. *The New India Museum, Whitehall Yard. From the* Illustrated London News, *3 Aug 1861.*

seeking this kind of entertainment preferred an outing to fresher air and the Crystal Palace. The Imperial Theatre, at the west end of the building, also suffered from an unfashionable location, at least until taken over by Lillie Langtry. She rebuilt it in 1901, two years before the Aquarium closed. In 1907 she sold the fabric to the developers of Central Hall. The remains, incorporated in the Dockland Music Hall in Canning Town, survived until destroyed by fire in 1931.

Westminster's most important theatre, though one which has a stronger link with music hall and vaudeville than with drama, is undoubtedly the Victoria Palace, which has a pedigree traceable to a pub of 1832. Here one John Moy began with 'select harmonic meetings', which developed, by way of a programme of concerts, into a conventional music hall bill. The premises were enlarged as the Royal Standard Music Hall by his successor in 1886. When demolished in 1911 for the present building this had become the longest-standing music hall in London. (In fact it did not become a regular home for drama until the 1930s.) Alfred Butt (who ran the 'mother' theatre, the Palace at Cambridge Circus) commissioned the design from the doyen of theatre architects of the period, Frank Matcham. Originally there was a figure of Anna Pavlova on the tower, an image which the dancer is said to have greatly disliked, and which has not reappeared since its wartime removal.

155. *The facade of the Imperial Theatre, from a 1901 souvenir brochure.*

PANORAMANIA

Perhaps Westminster's greatest curiosities were its two panoramas. In 1881 there was, with the installation of a circular painting of a battle scene, in a specially constructed building on the north side of Petty France, a revival of the panorama phenomenon which had transfixed the London public in Leicester Square and Regent's Park in the early years of the century. The Westminster (later, very grandiosely,

THE PROGRAMME

For MONDAY NEXT, DECEMBER 3rd

will include the following Artistes

GEORGIE WOOD
In a New Version of his Famous Sketch "THICKER THAN WATER"
Supported by DOLLY HARMER and FRANK LANGFORD

THE HOUSTON SISTERS
"The Irresistibles"

NORMAN LONG
"A Song, a Smile, and a Piano"

THE THREE WHIRLWINDS
A Sensation on Wheels

GUS FOWLER
The Watch King

THE VICTORIA GIRLS
Trained by Mrs. RODNEY HUDSON

MRS. WATERS' DAUGHTERS
(ELSIE & DORIS)
The Entertaining Entertainers

THE QUO VADIS BROS.
Roman Gladiators in a Unique Athletic Act

HAPPY SMART
The Famous Cabaret Eccentric Dancer from the Piccadilly Hotel

MATINEES ONLY   Commencing Boxing Day, Dec. 26th.
Doors open 1.45.   Commences 2.15.
Bert Coote presents a Children's Xmas Fairy Play

"THE WINDMILL MAN"
(Eighth Season)
By FREDERICK BOWYER

BERT COOTE AS "THE MAD GARDENER"

Prices : 7 - to 1 2 including Tax.

Phone : Victoria 5284 & 7358   Box Office Now Open 10 a.m.   9.30 p.m.

SEATS CAN NOW BE BOOKED

Have you seen Niagara Falls?
If not, go now to
NIAGARA HALL
Where the finest Panorama ever painted is on view.

ST. JAMES' PARK STATION
YORK STREET, WESTMINSTER
(Two minutes' walk from Westminster Abbey).

If you have, then revive your memories of the sublime
picture of Nature by visiting Niagara Hall, and see them
clothed in their beautiful Winter garments.

DAILY, 10 to 10.   ADMISSION, ONE SHILLING.

156. Victoria Palace theatre bill featuring 'Wee' Georgie Wood and Elsie and Doris Waters; 1934.

157. Advertisement for the Niagara Hall exhibition in Petty France (then called York Street), near St James's Park Station, 1888.

the National) Panorama consisted of a 16-sided polygon, inside which a gloomy passageway dimmed the spectator's vision until, ascending a staircase to a platform some 30 feet across, he or she was duly awed by the surrounding spectacle of distant fighting, the perspective enhanced by a gap of some fifty feet between the platform and the painting. The first offering here was historical, Castellani's painting of the battle of Waterloo, which had proved a major draw in Brussels; more newsworthy was its successor, the defeat of Egyptian rebels at Tel-el-Kebir in 1882. After several dark years, a theatrical impresario and journalist called John Hollingshead (who had failed to find a site on the fashionable side of the Park) brought here an American panorama of Niagara Falls, renaming the building Niagara Hall, employing native Americans to promote it, and annexing a

pub opposite for refreshment rooms. The final panorama, another view of Niagara by Edward Austen, remained on the walls when the panoramas closed as such in 1893, as backdrop to the Hall's eleven-year incarnation as a skating rink.

Yet another Waterloo extravaganza, in yet another National Panorama, opened in Ashley Place on part of the old Bridewell site in 1889. As Hollingshead had arranged at his Niagara Hall, the awesome but static spectacle was relieved by other attractions - not wigwams and their inhabitants this time, but phonograph demonstrations, 'Mrs Hunt's ladies' orchestra' and James Davey, a 'real Waterloo veteran' and presumably a natural showman, who would, according to the *Daily Graphic*, 'retail thrilling reminiscences to all comers, and fight his battles o'er again in fancy, in the pleasant evening of his age'.

158. A more conventional amusement: soldiers outside the Dove and Mitre in King Street, about 1875.

A Rainbow of Schools

GARRISONS AGAINST POPERY

The pious 17th-century founders of almshouses were usually also concerned, where funds allowed, to provide for the education of the young. Sometimes, indeed, optimism exceeded resources, so that it was many years before the founder's school was brought into being. Thus the brown coats of the children of Lady Dacre's Emanuel Hospital appeared only in 1738, nearly a century and a half from her endowment of the almshouses. The school endowed by Emery Hill in his will, opening its doors in 1817, post-dated his death by some 140 years. Palmer's Hospital, east of Brewer's Green, included a Black Coat School until 1728, when lack of funds forced this wing of the charity to close, not to open again for some ninety years.

In the meantime St Margaret's Hospital (the Green Coat School) had sprung out of local poor law provision in the 1620s. It was built near Artillery Row, seemingly in association with the initiatives which produced the bridewell and the workhouse. Despite rapid incorporation and royal patronage, the founders of the Blue Coat School and the Grey Coat School of the late 17th century must have found it appropriate to replicate it rather than enlarge it. The Blue Coat School sprang from the religious defensiveness of a group of worshippers at the Broadway Chapel, part of a late-17th century protestant backlash against Jesuit-led educational initiatives, begun in St Martin's and Covent Garden. The boys' school was founded in 1688, in Duck Lane (St Matthew Street), girls joining them in 1713 in the new building in Brewer's Green. The building was the gift of the brewer William Greene (he used the cellars for storing beer).

By contrast, the Grey Coat Hospital had its origin in the inability of the parish nurses, whom the authorities employed to look after orphaned or neglected children, to keep their young charges under

159. The Grey Coat School, photographed in the 1920s. The school was rebuilt in the 1950s after war damage (architect, Lawrence King).

160. *The Blue Coat School; watercolour by C.W. Dempsey c1860, showing Brewer's Green and the Two Brewers.*

161. *Printed music and text used at the Grey Coat School for grace before and after meat. Early 19th century.*

control. Parish children wandering up and down begging in the streets had appalled Emery Hill in the 1670s, and no less appalled the eight local shopkeepers who in 1698 founded a day school for 50 boys in the Abbey Sanctuary. They saw a clear link between the 'evil customs and habits' engendered in the children, especially their lack of religious instruction, and their probable 'shamefull and untimely death and Destruction'. Most of all, these children seemed to pose a threat to the parish peace and to its coffers, becoming 'the Curse and Trouble of all places where they live'.

Instruction proving fruitless while the children remained under the daily influence of those at home, the Grey Coat Hospital became a boarding establishment in 1701, moving into the old parish workhouse facing the Artillery ground, and admitting girls for the first time. The regime, which was typical of the charity schools, included basic instruction in English and the catechism, the children being trained primarily to take up apprenticeships in a suitable trade, or to go into domestic service. At first only those who were considered capable seem to have been taught to write and to 'cast accompt'.

By the mid-19th century the parents of the children at the endowed schools were more middle class, more articulate and critical than their early predecessors. The curriculum was criticised for over-emphasis on manual training, the discipline largely for its absence. The outcome of the Endowed Schools Commission of 1864, delayed partly on account of vigorous opposition from the City Corporation as governors of Emanuel, was a total reorganisation of the Westminster charity schools. In 1874 the Grey Coat Hospital became exclusively a girls' school, under church management. The Emanuel boys moved to Wandsworth in 1882. The other schools amalgamated as what is now the City of Westminster School, housed on what was originally the endowment land, later the garden, of Emanuel Hospital, fronting Palace Street.

162. *'An Internal view of Saint Margaret's Hospital, Westminster'. The Green Coat School, showing four of its scholars holding up the illustrative panel.*

WESTMINSTER SCHOOL

Westminster School has taught its scholars in the Abbey precinct literally from time immemorial. Though a date (1394) and a name (memorably, Henry Hum) can be found for the first master, no foundation date is known for the school itself, although it is believed to have originated to serve the Abbey, and from the beginning offered the instruction in the classics traditionally required for the learned professions. In the 16th century the school roll expanded from the original two dozen foundationers, and the college was re-founded by Queen Elizabeth: hence the assumption of the title of Queen's (or as the case may be King's) scholars. The 17th century is remembered for the rule of Dr Busby, whose scholastic achievements seem to have been marred by an inability to instil discipline. In the 1670s scholars were found larking about in Tothill Street at night, armed with swords, or consorting with the young women of the neighbourhood. One night when the good Doctor was at his country house in Chiswick, a party of scholars clubbed to death an unfortunate bailiff who had come to take possession of a house behind Dean's Yard. By this standard, throwing stones at the windows of the new church of St John the Evangelist in Smith Square, a pastime of some sixty years later, seems mere boyish high spirits.

The practice of going 'up Fields' for cricket had evolved by the mid-18th century, although not without fisticuffs when local teams made use of what the King's Scholars considered their exclusive pitches, in what is now Vincent Square. Individual sportsmen went fishing, and in winter skating, in the western ponds, including the grandiosely named King's Scholars' Pond, whose site is not precisely identified but was probably roughly where the northern end of Tachbrook Street now runs. There are accounts of snipe-shooting in the early 19th century; indeed, there was a gunsmith's conveniently situated in Marsham Street. Rowing was popular, although the boats were kept on the Lambeth shore. Increasing

163. *A Westminster scholar (1816).*

164. Westminster School c1840. From a watercolour by G.R. Sargent.

river traffic made rowing hazardous, and Searles' boathouse, which replaced Roberts's, disappeared on the extension of St Thomas's Hospital.

The annual Latin play, performed this century only intermittently, was instituted in the time of Henry VIII. In the 19th century the play became an event to which fashionable London society went to see and be seen. The New Dormitory, in which the play was latterly performed, was rebuilt on the site of the old (originally the Abbey granary) by the Earl of Burlington in 1722, adapting and 'correcting' plans originally developed by Wren and Hawksmoor. Although by the mid-19th century the mostly ramshackle premises and repellent neighbourhood of the school deterred fastidious parents, in increasing numbers, from committing their sons to its care, the Public Schools Commission of 1864 confirmed Westminster, in its view, as amongst the nine prime scholastic establishments in the country.

165. The Arch at Westminster School constructed in 1734; watercolour by A.G. Vickers, 1831.

166. *Drill for pupils of the Burdett-Coutts/Townshend School, c1916. The school was founded in 1876, from an endowment by the Revd Chauncey Hare Townshend, originally as a free evening institute for young working people. The Baroness Burdett-Coutts was an early trustee and supporter.*

INTO MODERN TIMES

Westminster provided for an elite; the charity schools, though evolving to provide for better-off pupils, could not keep pace with the growth of the 19th-century population. Ragged schools, such as that in the former One Tun pub in Old Pye Street, were established in the 1840s for the unfortunate children who, two centuries before, would have excited the concern of the charity school founders. In the 19th century, Pimlico and Westminster boasted between them about a dozen private academies at any one time. One of them, the Pimlico Grammar School, provided a classical education for boys for only a few years from 1830, but has left behind it the charming building at 22 Ebury Street. Every new church, district chapel and dissenting chapel had to have its satellite schools, dedicated to education of the local poor in the true faith. The majority were Anglican, like the Burdett-Coutts/Chauncey Townshend schools, but Roman Catholics and Wesleyans also made substantial provision. The National Schools movement of the established church, shrewdly staking out a central but economical location, had its training college in Victoria Street. Unkindly, the brown-coated pupils of Emanuel dubbed the National school in Dacre Street the Drab Coat School.

167. *Cookery class for boys at the Burdett-Coutts/Townshend School, c1916.*

When in 1870 the School Board for London came to be established, it appeared that Westminster was, considering the density and relatively low income of the bulk of its population, schooled reasonably effectively. In their first twenty years only three new schools were provided – in Horseferry Road, Buckingham Gate and St George's Row, followed shortly by a school on the new Millbank housing estate.

168. *Mr Gray's Academy, a private school in Great Smith Street, 1836. Interior view printed as part of a Leaving Certificate.*

169. *The Pimlico Grammar School, 22 Ebury Street, 1832.*

City Improvement

PARISH GOVERNMENT

The story of local government in Westminster before the end of the 19th century is of a patchwork pattern of specialised bodies.

The most important tasks of local government were accomplished at parish level. There were separate commissioners who dealt with drainage and paving, and later a burials board. But for most purposes, until 1855, local government - largely a matter of lighting, street-cleaning and the maintenance of a nightly watch - was the province of the select vestries of St Margaret, St John and St George. The area between Horseferry Road and Vauxhall Bridge Road was given to the Tothill Fields Trust, and the Grosvenor estate was the heartland of another trust, both set up in 1826. Until the Metropolitan Police were established in 1828 the parish authorities were responsible for law and order, and the facilities of the parish cage in St Margaret's churchyard often had to

be supplemented by taking space in the Gatehouse prison. The office of scavenger dealt with both street-cleaning and refuse collection, which in practice was contracted out on an annual basis, often to a local cowkeeper. St John's and St Margaret's were joined to form a poor law union after 1832, and after 1855 were drawn ever closer together for a range of administrative functions. Their headquarters, built in 1882, became Caxton Hall. Until the Metropolitan Fire Brigade was set up in 1866, the parish fire engines (St Margaret's being kept in the churchyard, and St John's in a special building on the corner of Regency Street) often competed with each other (and the private insurance companies) to be first on the scene of a fire. The St Margaret's team, having horsepower rather than merely manpower, usually won.

From 1855 the vestries were directly elected, and from 1900 formed part of the City of Westminster, borough status being granted by Parliament and City status claimed under a grant of Henry VIII. The new borough inherited initiatives of other ad hoc commissioners. In 1857 St Margaret's and St John's became sponsors of London's first free publicly financed library, taking over facilities first established

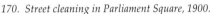

170. *Street cleaning in Parliament Square, 1900.*

171. *Firemen bringing out the engine at the Fire Station in Greycoat Place, c1907.*

172. *The City of Westminster Literary Scientific and Mechanics' Institution on the east side of Great Smith Street; engraving c1840.*

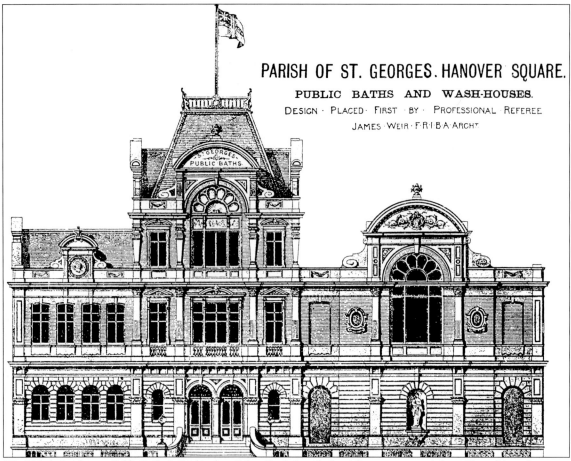

173. *This design for new Public Baths in Buckingham Palace Road, though placed first, was not carried out. The architect, James Weir, was here complementing the style of the Grosvenor Hotel. Instead, an Italianate, pedimented design by F.J. Smith was preferred by the vestry.*

174. *The Reading Room at the public library in Buckingham Palace Road*

in 1840 by a working men's self-help organisation called the Westminster Literary, Scientific and Mechanics' Institution, for which premises had been built on the east side of Great Smith Street. The united parishes were also among the first to build public baths, which were rebuilt in 1893 adjacent to the new library, on the opposite side of the street from the first one. By this time St George's had provided Pimlico with baths and a library, both in Buckingham Palace Road. St George's Baths were described by the City Council, as recently as 1950, as 'the leading public swimming bath in the Metropolis.' The Great Smith Street baths (now the Abbey Community Centre) was a much more modest affair, down to the 'second class entrance' from St Ann Street.

MANSIONS FOR ALL

In the last two decades of the 19th century the mansion flat came into its own. The pioneer, beginning in 1873, was one H. A. Hankey, the creator of Queen Anne's Mansions, with its eight storeys for long London's tallest building, and almost unanimously considered the ugliest of its age. (Architectural opinion nominated the Aquarium.) Hankey nevertheless appears to have succeeded in establishing a market for the upper-middle class flat, much imitated in the Victoria Street area and patronised (according to the incumbent of St Andrew's, Ashley Place) by a transient population. St Ermin's Hotel was originally serviced flats, with their own livery stables, division bell and private entrance to St James's Park Station. Ashley Gardens was first occupied in 1890, and St James's Court, Artillery Mansions and Westminster Palace Gardens followed. Amongst others which have now gone was the monumentally ugly Victoria

Street block which became the Army and Navy (later the Windsor) Hotel, and Members' Mansions in Broadway, the name proclaiming MPs as its intended clientele.

The demolition of the Millbank Penitentiary afforded the opportunity to build a gallery to house the national collection of British art, its nucleus the Turner bequest and the personal collection of the sugar refiner Sir Henry Tate. It also provided a site for implementing the London County Council's programme of rehousing people whose homes were being demolished for its street-widening programme in central London. The principle of publicly-financed housing had become established by 1890, and the Council was determined to build homes which, though still in five-storey blocks, were visually superior to the traditional model dwellings. The Millbank estate was completed in 1902. Though few of the flats had their own water supply or WC, and there were

175. *The Oriental Room in an apartment in Ashley Place, the residence of Major George Wallace Carpenter, c1893. Photograph by Bedford Lemere.*

176. *The boudoir in the apartment in Ashley Place of Major George Wallace Carpenter, c1893. Photograph by Bedford Lemere.*

177. *The LCC's Millbank Estate - Leighton and Millais Houses.*

179. *Artillery Mansions, 1895, designed by John Calder; a contemporary image designed to promote an up-market clientele.*

178. *Queen Anne's Mansions, looking west from Tothill Street to the top of Broadway, c1900. On the far corner on the right, the Hoop and Grapes and Old Star and Crown; on the front left, the St James's tavern, which disappeared with the reconstruction of the underground station in the late 1920s.*

180. City of Westminster Dwellings in Regency Street. Pencil drawing by Howard Penton.

no baths, there was a revolutionary attention to architectural decoration, in the modish arts and crafts manner, and the Houses were proudly named after painters whose work could be seen in the Tate Gallery alongside. The same careful approach to detail is evident in the contemporary Regency Street flats of the new borough council (illustration 180).

EDWARDIAN ENERGY

Since the 1870s the resident population had been in decline, which continued clearance and rehousing did nothing to reverse. But the daytime population was on the increase. From the turn of the century Westminster saw much of its ancient face disappear under massive and monolithic new office blocks built on a wholly unprecedented scale. King Street was swept away in 1898, offices in Victoria Street becoming sought-after as never before. What was left of the ancient streets between King Street and the Park went in 1900 for new offices, initially the home of the Local Government Board, later the Ministry of

Health. Parliament Square was once more enlarged, the new Middlesex Guildhall completed in 1913. There were still pockets of poverty; by the end of the century these were principally around Chadwick Street, and Lewisham Street off Storey's Gate. The Lewisham Street slum was eliminated by deliberately enlarging the ground taken for Central Hall, which rose in the place of the Aquarium. Central Buildings resulted as a by-product of the scheme. Parliamentary powers were taken by a private consortium to improve the courts and alleyways between Millbank and Marsham Street, demolishing the south and east sides of Smith Square. Palatial new offices resulted on one side of Millbank, and on the other the wharves were demolished and replaced by the Victoria Tower Gardens. A proposal to redevelop the Cowley Street area into an 'attractive residential quarter', perhaps along the lines of Little College Street, encountered influential opposition and was dropped, although individual houses have been sympathetically rebuilt.

BETWEEN THE WARS

Much rehousing was achieved after 1918. Tufton Street was transformed by the vision of the architect G. J. Cawthorne, who had previously modernised and rebuilt much of Catherine Street and Buckingham Place. He or his purchasers replaced ramshackle cottages with flats and new town houses of eclectic design. In 1922 the Peabody Trust built modern flats in Horseferry Road. The Grosvenor estate and the City Council co-operated on wiping out the Johnson development in the Page Street area, an existing scheme acquiring extra urgency when the river flooded, claiming the lives of residents on Millbank, on the night of 6th January 1928. The outcome was Lutyens's 'chequerboard' flats, opened in 1930. Housing conditions in Pimlico's smaller property were causing concern, mainly because as the leases of the houses aged the leaseholders had no incentive to tackle problems such as damp. Conditions around the site of the old Equitable gasworks in Pulford Street were the worst in the neighbourhood. Pulford Street is no more because a group of concerned Westminster residents formed a trust, and developed here, from 1929, the earliest of the Aylesford Street flats, on land purchased cheaply from the LCC. On the site of the Army Clothing Depot rose Dolphin Square, opened in 1937, with more than 1200 flats, and said to be the largest single block of its kind in Europe.

181. *The dead end alley of Lanes Cottages, demolished c1906 as part of the redevelopment of the Smith Square area. The alley ran north from Romney Street.*

182. *The back gardens of Catherine Street, demolished at about the same time.*

183. *Cottages in Page Street, 1928, photographed (like those below) for a report by Westminster's Medical Officer of Health. Their consequent demolition resulted in the Page Street estate.*

184. *Houses between Esher Street and Kensington Place, looking north to the Chartered Gas Works in Horseferry Road, 1928.*

Wartime and After

Close to the railway, as well as to the river and its industrial rim, Pimlico suffered in the Blitz as no other area west of Aldgate. Alderney Street took the first large-scale damage; 300 people lost their homes here in October 1940. Sutherland Terrace and a shelter under Dolphin Square were horrifically struck. A catalogue of incidents could only hint at the misery and the courage of the thousands of individuals involved, whether as victims or rescuers. The stations, and the riverside factories and warehouses did not escape. Buckingham Palace, the Abbey and the Palace of Westminster took as much if not more than their share. The devastating night of 10 May 1941, which accounted for a substantial part of Turner House on Millbank, three hotels in Vauxhall Bridge Road, the lantern of the Abbey, the tube line between St James's Park and Victoria, and most of the horses at the Stag brewery, also made the House of Commons temporarily homeless. One of the most terrible incidents occurred during the 'little blitz' of 1944, when a flying bomb fell on the Guards' chapel in mid-service, killing 119.

Post-war redevelopment has not been confined to renewal where bombs had fallen. Westminster's re-housing programme continued, the vast estate at Churchill Gardens - almost a small town - taking shape from 1946 on a site first earmarked for this purpose in the 1930s, and subsequently enlarged following extensive bomb damage in the area. Its completion, in 1962, coincided with the early stages of a striking new scheme, Lillington Gardens - the hanging gardens of Vauxhall Bridge Road, representing the reaction against modernism. Inevitably, industry and its attendant wharves have gone, no more than a handful of early Victorian frontages surviving, south of Vauxhall Bridge, to hint at what much of Millbank and Grosvenor Road once looked like. At the same time, residential Pimlico, having gone from genteel to shabby by reason of the combined effects of the leasehold system and rent restriction legislation, has in the last thirty years, through careful management, become once again one of London's most consistently desirable inner suburbs.

185. A Second World War machine-gun post in Parliament Square disguised as a W.H. Smith bookstall

186. Bomb damage in Alderney Street, October 1940.

187. Junction of Great Peter Street and Tufton Street, c1902. Between the beginning of the century and 1939 Tufton Street and Great Peter Street were entirely redeveloped.

*188. The British Overseas Airways terminal,
Buckingham Palace Road. The 1930s saw two
developments which greatly increased the importance of
the Victoria station area for transport: the coach
station, designed by Wallis Gilbert and Partners, 1931-2;
and the air terminal opposite, designed by A. Lakeman
(1939) and recently remodelled as the headquarters of the
National Audit Office.*

A falling population has also contributed to changes in the pattern of entertainment. While the Westminster Theatre (in the shell of Dr Dodd's chapel) and the Whitehall Theatre have since the 1930s sought metropolitan audiences, Victoria's pioneer cinemas, the Biograph of 1909 in Wilton Road, and the former 'News Theatre' (later a cartoon cinema) next to Platform 19 of Victoria Station have gone the same way as the Army and Navy Cinema of Strutton Ground. The remarkable foyer of the Metropole survives, however, as part of 160 Victoria Street, and the 'fairy cavern under the sea' (as the trade press described the Apollo Victoria, then the New Victoria, in 1930) lurks somewhere beneath the scaffolding of *Starlight Express*, which has played a substantial part in a minor renaissance of musical theatre round Victoria Station. But there is no working cinema left in the area.

The most dramatic changes have been in Victoria Street, where, beginning with the Stag brewery redevelopment in 1959, Victorian flats, chambers, and hotels, largely unloved, have given way to a parade of steel, glass and marble offices, charting the course of contemporary building fashion in much the same way as did the Victoria Street of the 19th century. The principal benefits have been, at long last, a properly dignified perspective for the formerly hemmed-in Cathedral, and the partial realisation of the street's potential as a shopping centre. Westminster City Hall, administering the greater Westminster created when the old borough was joined with Paddington and Marylebone in 1965, is one of a handful of skyscrapers which include the new New Scotland Yard and the Millbank Tower, first occupied by the Vickers company in 1964. There are unlikely to be more skyscrapers in the foreseeable future. Indeed, at the time of writing, the most unlovely of these products of the 1960s, the triple 'toast-rack' tower-slabs of the Departments of the Environment and Transport on the site of the old Horseferry Road gasworks, look set fair to crumble into Westminster past.

189. *The New Victoria Cinema auditorium, Oct 1930.*

Index

(asterisks indicate pages
on which illustrations
appear)